Captain John E Moore RN

The Soviet Navy Today

BOOK CLUB EDITION

This edition published by
Purnell Book Services Limited,
Milton Trading Estate, near Abingdon, Oxon.
by arrangement with Macdonald and Jane's Limited

Filmset in Monophoto Ehrhardt
by Tradespools Ltd, Frome

Printed in Great Britain by
Hazell, Watson & Viney Ltd, Aylesbury

Designed by Graham Marshall

CONTENTS

FOREWORD

The object of this book is to provide a form of reference on a navy which has grown from an ill-assorted bunch of ships with very little operational value to be one of the two most powerful navies in the world in under thirty years. In writing the text I have made every effort to avoid indulging in academic arguments and have tried to view the whole maritime affair from the realistic standpoint which is that of today's Soviet naval officer. Facts are the most important part and only where a consideration of the background is of value in placing these facts in their proper context have I offered rather more theoretical views. But "facts" does not mean the unrewarding task of counting numbers. In any fleet questions of morale and training must be uppermost in any consideration of capability. Alongside them estimates must be made of tactical knowledge, technical proficiency, whether a ship's company has the competence not only to get a ship to a given position but, once there, to keep it steaming, to keep its sensors functioning and its weapons able to be fired in the right direction if required. The greatest single factor is still the man, even in this era in which too many people look upon technology as the ultimate solution. It is the human brain which will continue to make the ultimate decisions and the value of any navy lies in that fact.

It is because I know that he agrees with this approach that I asked Professor John Erickson of Edinburgh University to provide an introduction. I am most grateful to him for this.

ERRATUM
The caption on page 85 should read ' "Victor" class '

INTRODUCTION

There can be no more apposite moment for the appearance of an up-to-date and highly professional assessment of the Soviet Navy than in the wake of the latest Soviet world-wide naval exercises, code-named Vesna (Spring) by the Russians themselves but generally described as Okean II (or Okean 75) by Western publicists out of a recognition of the continuity implied by a repeat, if somewhat enlarged performance of the original Okean manoeuvres conducted in 1970. Okean II, which lasted from 8 to 28 April 1975, involved at least 200 surface units, 100 submarines and substantial elements of the land-based Naval Air Force. These latest exercises were attended by maximum and deliberate publicity, in which the Western press duly lent its aid, though on this occasion the Soviet naval command played its own special part in advertising Soviet naval presence by transmitting orders *en clair*.

Though it is normal practice to think of the Soviet Navy in terms of its four geographically based fleets – the Northern, Baltic, Black Sea and Pacific – for the purposes of these exercises Soviet naval forces deployed into operational task forces, eight of which were committed and carried out missions in areas as widely separated as the Atlantic, the Mediterranean, the Pacific Ocean and the Indian Ocean – the latter an innovation on the 1970 exercises – and the Sea of Japan. More than seventy Soviet naval units were counted in the North Atlantic (an exceptionally high figure) and 100 in the North Sea and the Baltic. In addition to this obvious show of strength and the much publicised parade of naval power, these exercises displayed other unusual features, one of which was convoy manoeuvres on a large scale – with "convoys" being simulated by Soviet Navy supply and hydrographic or survey ships, or yet again by Soviet merchant ships requisitioned or under special charter for the duration of the fleet exercises. These "convoy operations" took place mainly off the Azores or in the Sea of Japan, while a Soviet hydrographic ship was deployed as a simulated "convoy" in the Eastern Atlantic. Since Soviet interest in their own convoyed shipping can only be minimal, in view of their general self-sufficiency, it can only be assumed that this phase represented a method of investigating attack procedures against

Western shipping. What lends credence to this view is the pattern followed by Soviet long-range naval reconnaissance aircraft, which flew tracks – Il-38s covering the Indian Ocean and the Northern Pacific, Tu-95s flying out of the Somalia base and from southern Russia as well as covering the Cuba-Conakry route – along and across the main Western shipping routes.

Yet another significant feature of these Soviet exercises in the Atlantic was the establishment of a substantial "blockade line" between Iceland and the Norwegian coast by Soviet submarines and the strategic inter-connection of the Atlantic-North Sea-Baltic was amply demonstrated by the unprecedented scale of the transfer of Soviet combat units from the Baltic to the Atlantic, thus practising rapid reinforcement of those Soviet forces committed to the interdiction of Western supply lines between North America and Europe. The aim of the exercise appears to have been to bring together powerful formations derived from the several fleets in the north, the Baltic and the Black Sea: if indeed there was some rehearsal of protecting their own shipping, much more manifest was the pressure which might be brought to bear against Nato's Atlantic com-munications. In addition, the Soviet naval command was obviously interested in testing how many of their forces could break through the Baltic outlets, through the Channel and the Denmark Strait – and in what time scale. The offensive role of the Naval Air Force was also demonstrated by more than seventy simulated attacks using anti-ship missiles.

While Soviet naval units, particularly those of the Baltic Fleet, ven-tured further to the west than ever before (even penetrating Lübeck Bay), the Soviet Navy operated for the first time under a single control centre for all missions in all ocean areas, a procedure facilitated and improved by Soviet ocean surveillance and communications satellites, whose orbital altitude is boosted finally to some 600 miles: the 65° inclination also per-mits the monitoring of ocean traffic reaching to latitudes within the region of the Arctic circle. With two satellites placed in orbit in close succession and at a boosted altitude, data on ocean movements can be transmitted to either ships or shore stations up to a range of 2,200 miles. Thus, the much advertised, indeed the deliberately advertised global reach and range of the Soviet Navy is matched by a high speed communications system with the requisite span and surveillance capability.

This, then, is the "new-look" Soviet Navy, no longer so closely geographically constrained and confined to purely defensive tasks but globally deployed and with a preponderance of submarines (built and building) which can only suggest an offensive anti-ship (whether naval or mercantile) role. It is not surprising, therefore, that such a parade of naval power induced a certain *frisson de terreur* in Western circles, not least among those very commentators who had themselves contributed to magnifying these capabilities. Numbers alone are not in themselves a conclusive argument and as Captain Moore very properly points out in his historical survey of Russian naval developments, both Imperial and Soviet Russia have always "ranked" high in the league of naval power in terms of numbers – a fact which may surprise many. Both regimes, Imperial and Soviet alike, have expended prodigious resources on the development of a navy and both have been guilty of arbitrary, if not fatal political interference in naval affairs: where there was not interference, more often than not apathy wreaked even greater havoc.

Throughout the long chronological span of Russian naval development a cyclical pattern of frenzied building programmes and intense interest in maritime matters has alternated with neglect, apathy and ignorance. The stupendous effort on the part of Peter the Great to build a navy was followed by decline and neglect, only to be followed by Catherine II's renewed interest and the onset of the "golden age" of Russian sea-power, with the quality of ships and men alike miraculously improved. Progress ended abruptly in 1815, to be followed by defeat, the challenge of advancing technology and yet another spasm of reform and re-organisation after 1905, the maritime martyrdom of Tsushima. What seems to have eluded the Imperial and Soviet regimes in their turn, however, is establishing an effective understanding of and relationship between naval capability and the pursuit of Russia's proper maritime interests or "mission". Latterly Admiral-of-the-Fleet of the Soviet Union, S. Gorshkov, has lectured his own navy and the Soviet leadership at large on the need to understand Russia's historical mission at sea and to assure Soviet naval power in a very comprehensive sense – its political potential, technical proficiency and tactical competence.

Building programmes, design features, organisation and deployment all form, of necessity, part of this programme, but as Captain Moore stresses from the outset "the man" – not technology alone – is decisive. That judgement is borne out by the present preoccupation of the Soviet naval command, which never ceases to press not only its professional training but also the "morale-psychological preparation" (to use the Soviet term) deemed essential for an ocean-going navy. The manpower policies of the Soviet Navy express at once its achievements and its weaknesses and here Captain Moore's own professional eye has lighted on both, without forgetting the relevance of what is called *morskaya kultura* – the seaman's innate skill and orderliness, ship-shape in every sense.

Okean II apart, though it obviously intrudes itself, this is the very juncture for an appraisal of Soviet naval power and the nature of the capability developed at sea, all without that naïvete which marks those who know nothing of Russia's maritime past or that gaucherie born of knowing too little of ships and the sea – a deficiency of *morskaya kultura*, in short. Captain Moore is neither dazzled nor derogatory and to this stance he can add the advantage of timeliness, whether the Soviet Navy continues on its present course or suffers one of those sea-changes brought about by yet another cycle in what has so far proved to be an arduous history and a perilous climb to the present eminence. Pre-eminence is altogether a different matter, as Admiral-of-the-Fleet of the Soviet Union S. Gorshkov would be the first to aver.

Professor John Erickson
Director of Defence Studies,
Edinburgh University

MOSKVA CLASS

KANIN CLASS

KARA CLASS

KASHIN CLASS

KRESTA II CLASS

KILDIN CLASS

KRESTA I CLASS

KRUPNY CLASS

KYNDA CLASS

KOTLIN CLASS

SVERDLOV CLASS

**KOTLIN CLASS
(WITH HELICOPTER PLATFORM)**

KRIVAK CLASS

SAM KOTLIN

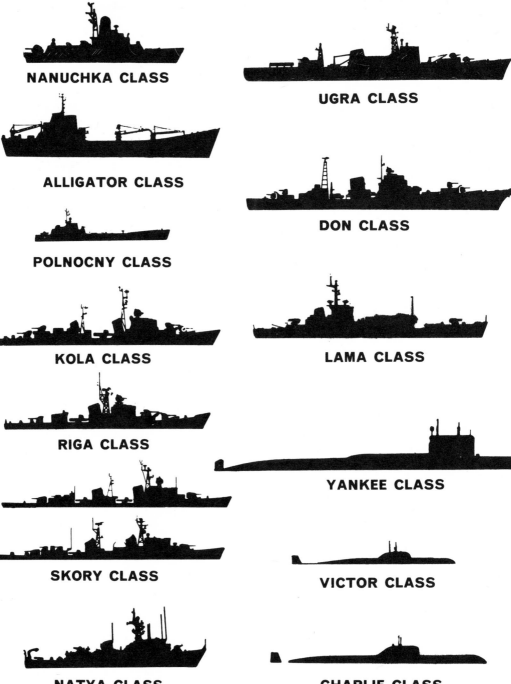

GRISHA CLASS

VANYA CLASS

NANUCHKA CLASS

UGRA CLASS

ALLIGATOR CLASS

POLNOCNY CLASS

DON CLASS

KOLA CLASS

LAMA CLASS

RIGA CLASS

YANKEE CLASS

SKORY CLASS

VICTOR CLASS

NATYA CLASS

CHARLIE CLASS

PART I

Growth of the Soviet Navy

Although the power of Russia has been centred on her land forces for centuries it is incorrect to state that she has no naval history. Certain of the nationalities which were eventually incorporated in All-the-Russias were active at sea eleven hundred years ago. The invasions of the Mongols, however, cut them off from the southern coasts and, in the Baltic, a tenuous hold in the Gulf of Finland was destroyed in the early 17th Century. All that was left was the inhospitable northern shores where exploration had followed in the wake of the spreading conquest of Siberia in the 16th and 17th Centuries. As Peter the Great pursued his task of reforming the state on Western lines so he built-up a fleet to contend with that of Sweden. Having obtained a foothold in the new town of St. Petersburg and on the off-lying Kotlin Island the Russians had a base and ship-building facilities. From here they moved to engage the Swedes off Hanko in 1714, a victory which, with two later and minor engagements, played an important part in the final conclusion of the war in 1721.

As was customary in the West peace brought decay to the naval forces and, though some resuscitation took place during the Seven Years War, it was not until the war with Turkey in 1768–74 that any further laurels came their way. The Battle of Cesme was a notable success and the peace saw the Russians once more moving into the Black Sea littoral. A Mediterranean force under Ushakov and, later, Senyavin operated for a number of years during the early period of the Napoleonic Wars, operations which were to be abruptly terminated by Russia's *volte-face* at the Treaty of Tilsit when she aligned her policy and forces with those of France. This was a period when the Aegean area took an important position in Russian strategic thinking, an interest which was to be shown at frequent intervals in later years. In 1827 she joined with the British and French in the destruction of the Turkish-Egyptian Fleet at Navarino. Six years later a second *volte-face* brought her to Turkey's aid and she obtained sole right of passage to the Black Sea in the Treaty of Unkiar Skelessi. This dominance was to last for only eight years and in the Crimean War (1853–56) the British and French fleets held unhindered passage through the Sea of Marmara. Since those days, the right of ships to make this passage has been frequently at issue, until today it is codified in the annexes to the Montreux Convention. Russia and, subsequently, the USSR has looked on the Eastern Mediterranean for 150 years as a desirable sphere of influence and in 1972 it was Admiral Gorshkov who bluntly stated, "Russia is a Mediterranean power. The location of its forces in these waters is based not only on geographical conditions, but also on the age-old need for the Russian fleet to stay there." It may be an "age-old need" in Russian eyes but only recently has their fleet been in a position to "stay there".

With what money was made available for the creation and sustenance of her 19th Century navy the High Command had to attempt to provide fleets which were independent in their own areas – the White Sea, the Baltic, the Black Sea and the Pacific. Inter-fleet reinforcement was a slow and costly business as was shown when Vice-Admiral Rozhestvensky led his fleet from the Baltic to the Pacific in 1904–05. After 18,000 miles of steaming, interspersed with lengthy pauses, his ships were reinforced by those of Rear-Admiral Nebogatoff and the great majority sunk or captured by the Japanese at the Battle of Tsushima in May 1905.

By 1904 the Russian navy was not only widely dispersed but it was ill-led, inadequately trained and of low morale. Although in straight numbers it ranked probably fourth in the world its ships were of poor quality, slow, badly protected and with artillery of indifferent design and efficiency. This deplorable situation was coupled with a lack of understanding of the fundamentals of sea power at the court, where power still lay. Although many individual attempts were made to progress in such fields as submarines, mining and torpedoes these achieved scant success through lack of understanding and support.

In the aftermath of the defeat by Japan and with a backcloth of a much-depleted Baltic Fleet, an antique Black Sea Fleet, the few remains of the Pacific Fleet and a non-existent Northern Fleet any decisive action appears to have been paralysed. It was not until 1907 that a strategic plan was agreed. This was an admirable start – the tasks of the various fleets were defined and plans drawn up to provide the ships to execute these tasks. It is clear that the German naval and military expansion was causing apprehension, because part of the Navy's role was to oppose any moves by the Kaiser's forces in the Baltic. Yet, despite this apprehension, the building programme was carried out with a procrastination and dilatory execution which ensured that only one of the planned capital ships was completed by the time war broke out. While British battleships were being completed in two years and those of Germany in three it was taking at least five years to achieve the same result in Russia. Not surprisingly the Russian fleet ranked eighth amongst the world's maritime powers in *Jane's Fighting Ships* (1914 edition).

During the war from 1914 to 1917 the Russian Navy played an un-distinguished role and it was only from the time of the October Revolution in 1917 that it appeared in the headlines. It was the sailors of the Baltic

Fleet who had a major part in the revolution in the St. Petersburg area and it was the signal gun of the cruiser *Aurora* which started the assault on the Winter Palace in which the majority of Kerensky's provisional government was sheltering. On the rivers and lakes the navy took up arms against those opposing the revolution but this was confined to the Baltic region. The German capture of Sevastopol in May 1918 caused the scuttling of a large number of the Black Sea Fleet, a process which was continued later by ships' companies opposed to the Bolsheviks. In the Pacific area Admiral Kolchak led the forces opposed to Lenin's government and, in February 1921, a rising in St. Petersburg was fomented by naval elements who were demanding free elections and the easing of Bolshevik controls. The result was predictable – a large number of those concerned were incarcerated in the forerunners of today's labour camps. Soviet commentaries on this period stress the decision of the 10th Party Congress, held in March 1921, to "take measures toward the revival and strengthening of the Red Navy". This was not before time if there was to be any intention of providing a naval force for the new state – in a year its tonnage had fallen to a quarter of the previous total and these ships were manned by a sixth of the manpower of early 1920. The latter figure is the more significant for not only does it include a dramatic dilution amongst the ratings but the loss of a high proportion of the experienced officers on whom the burden of training would fall. Political reliability was essential if the Bolsheviks were to be certain of the allegiance of the newly planned fleet and the inclusion of political commissars in all aspects of naval affairs was designed to achieve this. The recruitment of large numbers of the Communist Youth Organisation, Komsomol, played its part in ensuring the adherence of the navy to the government's cause.

The provision of ships for both the navy and the merchant marine was seriously delayed by the extensive damage to the shipyards during the war. Although the rebuilding of these yards was begun in 1921 the majority of vessels had to be provided from the refit and reconditioning of those remaining from Tsarist times. By 1924 two battleships, one cruiser, eighteen destroyers and nine submarines were ready and the result was the reforming of small squadrons in the Baltic and Black Seas as well as the inauguration of detachments of small craft on the Caspian and the Amur River. By 1926 sufficient shipbuilding capacity was available for a new-construction programme of twelve submarines, eighteen escort vessels and thirty-six light craft to be approved by the Defence Council. This was designed to provide new forces for national defence which was, at this time, founded on the principle of short-range ships operating with the army and air force in areas defended by mines and coastal artillery. The First Five Year Plan of 1928 laid emphasis on submarine construction and this legitimised the laying-down in March 1927 of the first of the "Dekabrist" class of 1,300-ton submarines. The escort vessels of 1926 were never heard of again. From 1930 to 1934 the "Leninets" minelaying submarines, the "Shchuka" and "S" classes of about 900 tons and the much smaller "Malutka" class submarines began to join the fleet. The period of the First and Second Five Year Plans saw the ascendancy of the doctrine of defence and the craft designed to execute it.

But not all the building effort was applied to submarines. In the Second Five Year Plan surface ships were included – proposals were agreed for the construction of four cruisers of the 8,800-ton "Kirov" class, a number of the 3,500-ton French-designed "Leningrad" class destroyers as well as smaller escorts, minelayers, minesweepers and river gunboats. In 1938, after considerable behind-the-scenes activity and as Stalin's 1937–39 purges eliminated a large section of senior naval officers who might have opposed him, the decision to build a large ocean-going fleet was announced. This was to include battleships, heavy cruisers, light cruisers and destroyers as well as a considerable number of smaller ships. Later in the Third Five Year Plan (1938–43) aircraft carriers were to be added to the list, whilst the steadily mounting number of submarines was to be increased.

By the time Germany invaded Poland on 1 September 1939 the Soviet fleet was taking on a completely new aspect. One hundred and sixty-five submarines were in commission, all but eight being of modern design and construction, giving her an enormous preponderance over her German ally who possessed only fifty-seven boats on the same date. By the time this alliance was broken by Germany's invasion of Russia on 22 June 1941 the latter had 219 ships on the building slips – including three battleships, twelve cruisers, forty-five destroyers and ninety-one submarines – and approximately 275 in commission – three old battleships, ten cruisers, sixty destroyers (twenty being aged), 180 submarines and an assortment of light craft. The main body of this fleet was based in the Baltic, a substantial proportion in the Black Sea, some twenty destroyers in the Far East and ten destroyers forming the genesis of the Northern Fleet. This was basically in line with the strategic precepts laid down in 1907 for, after all, the Soviets were facing the same enemy in a different guise.

The impossibility of reconciling the bombastic claims and statements of Soviet historians with the more sober reports of their Western counter-parts underlines the problems of cooperation which existed between the two sides of the Alliance. Official Soviet sources claim that during the Great Patriotic War their navy sank 1,200 combatants and auxiliaries as well as 1,300 transports of 3,000,000 tons. The Western figures for these operations, as quoted in the British Official History of the War, are 114 surface warships of all types, none of which was sunk by major surface action but most by aircraft, seven U-boats and 214 merchant vessels of 445,526 tons. The round numbers of the Soviet list suggest a "ballpark" figure and it is, of course, possible that it includes small craft such as launches. However the comparable figures achieved by the Western navies in the area from Archangel to Gibraltar and 350 miles west of Europe, of 973 surface ships, 692 U-boats and 1,821 merchant ships sunk or captured between 3 September 1939 and 8 May 1945 suggests that the Soviet totals are somewhat inflated. In addition to this the grand total of 321 German naval vessels listed in Weyer's Taschenbuch der Kriegs-flotten for 1940 would have required a prodigious building programme, of which the Germans were incapable, to provide enough ships for these Russian figures to have any veracity.

The reasons for what was a comparatively poor showing in these four years were evident to those who met and worked with the Soviet navy at this time. Basically designed as a coast-defence navy and having had little opportunity to adjust to Stalin's instructions to operate as an ocean-going fleet, robbed of the majority of its experienced officers in the pre-war purges and with inadequate technical backing or training it is hardly surprising that little of note was achieved. Over 400,000 sailors were transferred to land-fighting and the main successes resulted from the operations of river-flotillas, particularly in the south under the command of Rear-Admiral Gorshkov.

Heavy losses were incurred, largely from air attacks. By May 1945 some half of the surface ships had been sunk, a number of submarines lost and the naval building programme was almost totally destroyed, along with the major building slips and dockyards. Training had been virtually at a stand-still and the fleet had been drained of so many ratings to support the army, a task in which they served with much gallantry, that the post-war years called for a major effort in re-manning as well as re-building

It is worth considering the state of Soviet naval technical efficiency in 1945. A number of their ships were of foreign design but lacked modern equipment. Their sensors were of little use, radar having been dis-covered for the first time with the incorporation of foreign ships in their fleet and sonar being similarly strange to them. Fire-control was in-efficient and this was true of most other aspects of naval technology. Standards of reliability of both propulsion and weapon-systems were inadequate although these were under comparatively little strain in the brief sorties which were the normal type of operations undertaken.

Nor did these short periods at sea give much opportunity for tactical training. With inefficient sensors and weapons the Soviet naval officer was in no position to excel in the manner in which his Western counter-parts, with extended periods at sea and backed by technology much further advanced than in the USSR, were able.

But the immediately succeeding years were to show that he could learn and learn fast. With the coming of peace came also an influx of ideas from captured German scientists and technicians, backed by the evidence of the ex-Nazi ships and submarines which were incorporated in the Soviet fleet. Whilst the building of pre-war classes of submarines and the com-pletion of a number of cruisers and destroyers went ahead under Stalin's instruction of July 1945 to provide a fleet "still stronger and more powerful", new designs were on the drawing-board. The Soviet shipyards had pioneered the building of submarines in sections which were later to be welded together, a method much used by the Germans in their vast submarine construction-programme. By 1950 this method was being used in the building of the first post-war designed "Whisky" class submarines. This was a derivation from the German Type XXI design which, though smaller than the German boats was capable of an underwater speed of 15 knots. Larger, too, was the USN's "Tang" class which achieved a slightly better performance on 2,700 tons (dived) and for which it had taken the same time to assimilate the lessons of the German boats. But with the designs of the first nuclear submarine in hand, only six of the "Tangs" were built — the USSR turned out 240 of the "Whiskys" between 1951 and 1957. Almost simultaneously a programme of twenty-five "Zulu" class, a larger and longer-range version of the "Whiskys" with three shafts and four more torpedo tubes was put in hand.

This particular programme has been emphasized because it illustrates a trend in Soviet naval methods. Once a class has been designed there is normally no delay in the proving of a prototype – the class is put into series production forthwith. Any subsequent changes required can be incorporated later in a conversion or modernisation programme. This has been evident in the alterations carried out to a number of submarines, in some cases resulting in a change of role, and in a number of destroyers and corvettes. Whilst in the past such modifications have usually been the result of availability of new weapons there now appear to be alterations caused by changes in tactical thought. These will be considered in more detail in later discussion of the various types.

A study of the various building programmes illustrates the changes which took place in Soviet naval thinking. As a result of her advances during the war the USSR was in a much stronger geographical position than before. She was entrenched in Poland and East Germany as well as Latvia, Lithuania and Estonia, an advance of some 700 miles towards the Baltic exits which included many important base-ports and shipbuilding facilities. In the Black Sea the adherence of Romania and Bulgaria provided friendly ports to within 150 miles of the Bosphorus entrance. The alliance with Yugoslavia and Albania gave her the longed-for foothold in the Mediterranean which she had tried, unsuccessfully, to extend to Greece during the civil war there in 1946–49. In the Far East, as a result of her twenty-five days at war with Japan she had lodgement in the Kuriles, the whole of Sakhalin, North Korea and Manchuria. All of this geographical advance provided valuable forward bases for any further expansion which might be planned in the future.

But that was to be some years ahead. In 1945 the USSR was counting the cost of the Great Patriotic War – 20 million dead and the loss of a third of her economy. Defence was the immediate need, a shield behind which recovery could be pressed ahead with all speed. The continuing submarine programme has already been mentioned, a programme in which the emphasis was placed on medium-range boats, the majority of which were to be based on the coast lines of the Baltic and the Black Seas. From these areas egress to the open oceans was restricted by the Danish and Turkish straits and deep-sea operations far from base would have been precluded by the lack of support ships.

The surface ships of the immediate post-war period were conventional in their design and capabilities, well suited for simple defensive operations. Seven cruisers and a number of destroyers of pre-war design were completed and then the emphasis swung to two new classes – the "Sverdlov" cruisers and the "Skory" destroyers. The first of these, 19,200-ton ships with twelve 6-inch guns and a speed of 34 knots, were to be the backbone of the fleet, valuable in defence as well as possessing a considerable offensive capability. Twenty-four were originally planned but for reasons we shall see only fourteen were completed. Eighty-five "Skory" class, large destroyers of 3,500 tons armed with four 5.1-inch guns and ten torpedo tubes and capable of 36 knots, were projected, although only seventy were completed between 1949 and 1954.

By the early 1950s the third of the four elements of defence (surface and submarine forces, aircraft and coast-defence weapons) was strengthened to 4,000 aircraft. Over half were comparatively modern fighters whilst the remainder were *Badger* long-range jet aircraft with the first air-to-surface weapons, *Beagle* torpedo-bombers and a miscellany of reconnaissance, A/S and liaison machines. The Soviet Naval Air Force had not yet gone to sea and was provided only with the means of defending surface forces within a few hundred miles of their bases, missile attacks on enemy forces out to the Iceland-Faroes gap or torpedo attacks in the northern part of the Norwegian Sea. It was in 1956 that the reinforcement of the *Bear* aircraft, fitted for reconnaissance or strike out to a radius of 3,500 miles without refuelling, provided a capability beyond that of pure defence.

In November 1957 the Russian Sputnik, the first earth satellite, gave the Western countries evidence of the vast strides taken by Soviet technology in the twelve years since the war. Yet a Western observer allowed full clearance would have found this advance clearly shown in the Soviet Navy. Two years before *George Washington*, the first US nuclear-propelled ballistic-missile submarine, was laid down in 1957 the Soviets had launched their first submarine-oriented ballistic missile. Admittedly the weapon itself, the *Sark* with the SSN-4 system, had a range of only 350 miles but it was enough. In 1956 the first "Zulu V" class diesel submarine was at sea, fitted with two ballistic-missile tubes in the fin. In 1958 the "Golf" class with three launchers was followed closely by the nuclear-propelled "Hotel" class with the same weapon load. The Soviets had scooped the pool. Following a decision which must have been made at least by 1950 they had produced a capability so far unknown and unmatched in Western navies. It was to remain this way until on 30 December 1959 *George Washington*, carrying sixteen 1,100-mile Polaris missiles, was commissioned. Thus by 1956 the USSR had affirmed its intention of moving into the international, inter-continental naval sphere. Although the range of the missiles left their carriers wide-open to a concentrated A/S defence the point was made.

All these plans were under development whilst the Korean War (1950–53), inspired and prompted by Stalin, had occupied the attention of all the major powers and a number of minor states. So far as naval affairs were concerned the United Nations held almost total supremacy at sea, largely due to the presence of strong forces from the USN and the Royal Navy. This display of the value of sea-power was reflected in the building programmes of the two navies, the former putting in hand new aircraft carriers which were soon to have a nuclear-delivery capability whilst the latter started its first post-war frigate replacement programme as well as a very large concentration on new minesweepers. The first of these, the carriers, was soon to produce a reaction in the Soviet navy's own reconstruction efforts.

The death of Stalin in March 1953 and the end of the Korean War very shortly afterwards resulted in major changes of emphasis. The Allied fleets returned from the North-West Pacific at a time when the Kremlin leadership was in dispute. The emergence of Khrushchev as the eventual successor to supreme power brought a fundamental change in naval policy. Having set his face against a big-ship navy he installed Admiral Gorshkov, a comrade from his war-time days in Southern Russia, as the new C-in-C. This was an appointment which was to have far-reaching results. Whilst accepting the removal from the active list of over 300 warships and a halving of the Naval Air Force he very soon showed his political abilities. No doubt recognising a need to modernise his fleet, an aim which the Khrushchev cuts would facilitate, he contrived to salvage fourteen of the "Sverdlov" cruisers from the ban. The remainder of the classes which appeared in the twenty years of the Gorshkov era deserve rather closer examination.

Construction of the first class of this period, the "Krupny" missile-armed destroyers, probably started in 1957, the year after the new C-in-C took charge. This does not mean that the design was agreed at that time. Up to eight to ten years are frequently required in Western navies between the inception of a ship's design and the first of class being commissioned. This lead-time results from the frequent original discussions of the staff requirements, the production of sketch designs followed by enormously detailed shipbuilders' drawings, the ordering and supply of the multitude of components and, finally, the problems of actually building the first ship. In the case of the "Krupny" class some of these problems may have been minimised because of her considerable similarity to the four ships of the "Tallin" class completed in 1954. The hulls were very similar in size and conformation, the engines almost identical. The great difference was, however, the fitting of surface-to-surface (SSN-1) missile launchers both forward and aft. With initial delivery in 1959 and allowing for the possible reduction in lead time already discussed it is likely that the design was begun in 1952–53, just as the first of the new US *Forrestal* class carriers were laid down. Eight of the "Krupnys" were delivered in the period 1959–61, ships which were limited by their radar capability to engage only one target at a time with their missiles and, because of their lack of any long-range AA defence, required air cover to protect them. They were, however, capable of acting as a defensive force of considerable potential within the limits stated and remembering the fact that their 150-mile missiles probably required mid-course guidance at maximum range. Similar disadvantages existed in the design of the "Kildin" class which was slightly smaller than the "Krupny" being a conversion of the 415-foot "Kotlin" class hull. This class of four ships became operational at about the same time as the "Krupnys" and these were the last destroyers to carry surface-to-surface missiles until the arrival of the "Krivak" in 1971.

From 1962 onwards the main weight of surface-to-surface missile armament was put in cruisers of the "Kynda" class (1962–65), "Kresta I" class (1967–69), "Kresta II" class (1969 onwards) and "Kara" class (1973 onwards). These vary in size from the 6,000-ton "Kyndas" to the 10,000-ton "Karas" but all mount surface-to-air missiles as well as having helicopter facilities, and possess reasonable A/S capabilities. The steady improvement in their capabilities, in their ability to operate away from shore-based air cover, in their carrying helicopters able, in some cases, to act as reconnaissance and mid-course guidance machines reflects a fundamental change in policy. Allowing for a six-year lead time this whole programme may be a reflection of Admiral Gorshkov's determination to produce a fleet capable of world wide operations.

The other branch which provided for missile attacks on surface-ships was that of the submarines. The first to be at sea with cruise-missiles embarked were the "Whisky Twin Cylinder" conversions carrying a pair of SSN-3 launchers which were elevated from the after-casing. This 1958–60 modification was immediately followed by the "Whisky Long Bin". This more efficient variant had four launchers mounted in the fin and the "Juliet" class, apparently custom-built for this role, had pairs of launchers forward and abaft the fin. The first "Juliet" appeared in 1962 and, although the Twin Cylinders may have been test-beds for such operations, it seems more likely that the whole programme was aimed at the nuclear-strike carriers of the USN and RN. The first aircraft carrier to be propelled by nuclear power was laid down in 1958 – USS *Enterprise*. Her power plant gave her a maximum speed of 35 knots, similar to her non-nuclear opposite numbers, but allied with other nuclear-propelled ships such as *Long Beach* and *Bainbridge* she could form the core of a task force with almost unlimited range. Diesel-driven submarines such as the "Juliet" and her predecessors were in no condition to counter such a force and it seems most likely that the next cruise-missile submarine, the "Echo I", was a reaction to this threat. These five boats were, like the similar "November" class fleet submarines, nuclear-propelled and thus had the required endurance although their speed was no match for *Enterprise*. They were armed with six SSN-3 missiles in elevating launchers and must surely have been a makeshift to cope with the situation until the lead time for custom-built submarines was run off. The fact that all of the "Echo I" class have now been withdrawn from service or converted to normal fleet submarines tends to support this. With the design of the "Echo I's" successors, the "Echo II" class, in hand the construction of the "Juliet" class was cut by nearly a half and the rate of building slowed right down to about three a year from a possible twelve. By 1963 the "Echo IIs" were being commissioned, a total of twenty-seven being built in the next four years. They had an improved hull design and power plant and represented a major threat to surface forces. The long range (300 miles) of the SSN-3 missiles was necessitated by the submarines' need to surface before launch. This difficulty was overcome in the next class, the "Charlie", the first of which was delivered in 1967. These 5,000-ton submarines had a new hull-form, the third type evolved, better machinery and a speed in excess of 30 knots. But, most important, their SSN-7 missiles could be launched from dived. The firing range was reduced dramatically to 30 miles and a force commander opposed by these submarines was now faced with a very complicated A/S problem – "Echo" class at long-range, "Charlie" class at medium range and torpedo-carrying nuclear submarines closer in. Add to this fact that the "Echos" and "Charlies" also carried torpedo armament and one can see that the Soviet reaction to the carrier problem had been swift and effective. By the end of the 1960s they had a submarine force of such varied capabilities and huge numbers that they could not only act as a defensive screen for the homeland but also operate against the sea lanes of the world. In the fifteen years since Admiral Gorshkov's appointment they had outrun the West in numbers of submarines and had achieved parity with other navies in many operational aspects.

We have already seen the emphasis placed on the Naval Air Force in the immediate post-war years and the great reductions made in its numbers after Stalin's death. From then on major importance was placed on reconnaissance and air-to-surface strike. The *Badgers*, new in 1954, have provided the main strength of this force ever since. Armed with *Kipper*, *Kelt* or *Kerry* surface-to-air missiles they currently (1975) number about 300. Now they are probably being supplemented by the variable-geometry *Backfire* which is expected to carry a new 400-mile range air-to-surface weapon with low-altitude capability in 1976. Providing the very long-range reconnaissance and strike capability needed by a navy without major aircraft-carrier capability are the Tu-95 *Bears*, huge machines able to operate in a number of roles such as bombing, air-to-surface missile attack, mid-course guidance for ship or submarine launched missiles, as well as normal reconnaissance. In the recent major Soviet naval exercise, Okean 1975, these aircraft were employed on missions which took them to Cuba, Conakry (Guinea) and the Arabian Sea.

Backed by Il-38 *May* reconnaissance aircraft flying from Somalia and the Soviet Pacific coast these aeroplanes covered a large area of the world's oceans.

As well as these large fixed-wing aircraft there are not only a large number of A/S and communication aircraft but also an increasing number of over 100 helicopters. A large proportion of these are the Ka-25 *Hormone* which provide the major part of the Soviet Navy's embarked helicopter force. While facilities for rotary-wing aircraft were being built into the changing pattern of the cruiser programme plans were prepared for a totally new type of ship – the helicopter cruiser. Two of these were completed at Nikolayev in 1967 and 1968, *Moskva* and *Leningrad*. Of 18,000 tons full load these may have been the first of a continuing class whose production was cancelled. The reasons for such a decision could have been an increasing awareness of the need for embarked fighters in a force at sea coupled with the success of trials of the Soviet VTOL aircraft *Freehand*, a realisation that if an intervention capability was to be achieved fixed-wing aircraft would be required or a conscious move away from such a specialised type of ship. Whatever the reason, and one must not forget that cost-effectiveness is as well-recognised in the USSR as elsewhere, these were the only two ships with a flight-deck built for the Soviet navy until the "Kuril" class 35,000-ton aircraft carrier *Kiev* appeared. Although this ship is called an "Anti-submarine Cruiser" by the Russians this is as much a euphemism as other type-classifications used in certain Western navies. She is undoubtedly an aircraft carrier designed to operate both helicopters and VTOL aircraft, and represents the penultimate stage in the development of Admiral Gorshkov's "balanced Fleet".

Having dealt briefly with the evolution of the various types of ship in the Soviet Navy it is worthwhile to consider the political and international background to this unprecedented expansion, because there are a number of points in history which appear to have prompted or reinforced a change in policy. The decision to strive for a "big-ship navy" was taken by Stalin in time for its inclusion in the Third Five Year Plan starting in 1938. This was in the midst of the Spanish Civil War which had started in July 1936 and in which the USSR had chosen to play a part as the supporter of the Republican cause. With no land contact between Russia and Spain the majority of stores, armaments and "volunteers" had to be ferried thither by sea. But the sea was dominated by Franco's navy and by those of his allies, Germany and Italy. Interception and sinkings were very much on the cards and there was no way in which the Russians could protect their ships. A need for sea-power to back up foreign intervention was made very clear to the Kremlin.

Despite the belittling by Soviet historians of Western naval operations during the Second World War the lessons must have been apparent to the few competent senior officers who had survived the purges – the importance of aircraft and submarines, the demise of the battleship, the vital place of A/S warfare, the tremendous potential of amphibious operations, to list only a few. But nothing could be done to capitalise on these lessons until the shipyards were available and new designs had been prepared. So the late 1940s were a time for the continuation of the interrupted pre-war programmes in whatever yards had survived.

By 1950 the two main requirements were to hand and new classes appeared, still oriented very largely on defence. As the Korean war dragged on there was no place in it for Soviet intervention. Ship designs altered progressively and imaginatively but when, in October–November 1956, the combined Anglo-French-Israeli assault on Egypt took place the USSR had insufficient naval power to intervene on behalf of their associate, Nasser. Marshal Bulganin made threats of nuclear retaliation on London and Paris but there was no fleet to interfere with the very large forces grouped off Suez.

The same was true when President Chamoun of Lebanon requested assistance from the USA in the face of a possible *coup d'état* fomented by Syria and Egypt with Russian financial backing. The call was made on 14 July 1958 and from the following day until the end of October American forces were present in and around Beirut, effectively preventing the overthrow of a friendly government by foreign powers. No response by the Soviet navy was possible but 1958, although it brought this major diplomatic defeat for the USSR, was significant in other respects. The ships then completed were of little more than improved war-time design, but in that year the new navy was begun. New classes were laid down incorporating many of the technological improvements then to hand and the Red Fleet was on the way to becoming a force designed by, and reliant upon, its own people.

By 1962, before the 1958 programme changes had had full effect but when the USSR could deploy both ballistic- and cruise-missile submarines, nuclear-propelled fleet submarines, a vast force of diesel submarines and the early missile-armed surface ships, Khrushchev looked abroad. Maybe he believed that his policy of major reliance on submarines had provided adequate naval defence for Russia, maybe the wish to move into the further seas, which was apparently in the minds of some members of the higher command at this time, had urged him forward, maybe he thought the young President Kennedy was good for a bluff. None of these may be the right reason – all may have had some effect. What is certain is that in choosing his point of adventure he selected the most advantageous place for his purposes but totally misjudged the American reaction to his selection. Cuba had welcomed Fidel Castro on New Year's Day 1959 and, although his steady progression to the Left and his ever closer ties with the USSR did not endear him to many of his countrymen the fiasco of the landings in The Bay of Pigs in April 1961 showed that this lack of enthusiasm did not extend to violent opposition. Any affection for the USA was much diminished by the declaration of an embargo on US–Cuban trade in February 1962.

Castro and his country were friendless amongst the major states of his hemisphere and a wide open door was presented to the Russians. They hurried in with airborne and ground-launched missiles, trucks, troops and transporters, clearly intending to stay. Then came the dramatic events of the thirteen days of crisis after the American discovery of the missile sites, the careful steps by which President Kennedy increased the pressure on Khrushchev, the presence of a steadily mounting number of US ships, the forcing to the surface of all the Soviet submarines in the area, culminating in the final Soviet climb-down on 28 October. Three weeks later the American blockade was lifted and a totally unnecessary piece of "brinkmanship" had been circumvented. This incident has been discussed at some length because there were major lessons in it for both sides. The Western countries saw the danger of giving the Russians half-a-chance, for whatever reason, to establish themselves in a country that had been led or forced to their side. From the Soviet point of view there were the twin lessons that sea-power could thwart their purposes unless they held a preponderance in the area.

After 1962 Khrushchev adopted an increasingly conciliatory tone to the West, signed the Partial Nuclear Test Ban Treaty in 1963, and paved the way for a final break with China. By October 1964 he was, however, sufficiently discredited in his domestic and foreign policies for Brezhnev, with the assistance of Kosygin, Podgorny and others, to lever him out of the driving seat.

The naval situation inherited by Brezhnev was at a most interesting stage. The USN had twenty-eight ballistic missile nuclear submarines (SSBNs) in commission, the Royal Navy had laid down the first of the *Resolution* class SSBNs and France had the first *Le Redoutable* class SSBN on the slips. All these boats were equipped with missiles of over 1,000 miles range, and the USSR "Yankee" class, then building, was similarly armed. But the only Soviet SSBNs available were the "Hotel" class with 700-mile SSN-5 missiles, a range which made then vulnerable to A/S search in the long run to their possible launching areas. The Soviets were, therefore, still reliant upon the Strategic Rocket Forces for their nuclear deterrent, although by 1968 the arrival of the first "Yankees" would alter this balance. These were formidable craft of 9,000 tons carrying sixteen launching tubes for the 1,300-mile *Sawfly* (SSN-6) missiles. The knowledge of this particular building programme must have been some comfort to the Soviet hierarchy – with their superior building rate (one nuclear submarine per month) they must have known that by the late 1960s they would be in a position to threaten all the major capitals of the world.

The surface situation was still one in which the West's aircraft carrier strength was opposed by an immense Soviet submarine force armed with nuclear-headed torpedoes and cruise missiles. Close defence had been greatly improved by the very large building programme of "Osa" and "Komar" class missile-firing fast attack craft, lethal in normal sea-states out to a range of about 20 miles. Beyond their operating range the missiles were carried in cruisers and destroyers whose numbers, though low, were to be supplemented in the next few years by larger cruisers of the "Kresta I" class, then building at the Zhdanov yard in Leningrad.

This was no occasion for major adventures involving naval forces but the time was at hand to move from the confines of coastal waters to the high seas. The US carriers had already drawn the Soviet defences out to the Iceland-Faroes gap, and the problems of Cyprus, with their Turkish-American overtones, had resulted in the dispatch of a Soviet cruiser and two destroyers to the Mediterranean in mid-1964. In early 1963 Admiral Gorshkov had very clearly stated a policy of accustoming his fleet to oceanic operations, a public statement of a sentiment which must have been affecting his plans for some years.

Out-of-area deployments (away from local fleet areas) had started some years earlier. Visits to Indonesia in 1959 followed port visits in Europe. "Whisky" class submarines had been based in Albania until, in 1961, a reversal of policies in that country resulted in the departure of some of these boats and the detention of another two who joined a previous pair of the same class in the local order-of-battle.

In the ensuing years the Soviet naval ensign became more widely displayed: 1967, a major Soviet reinforcement of the Mediterranean group; 1968, a flag-showing squadron to eight countries in the Indian Ocean; 1969, the first Soviet squadron visit to the Caribbean and Cuba; 1970, the arrival of Soviet destroyers off Conakry in West African Guinea. These were all symptoms of a wide-reaching Soviet naval move into the outer oceans which was to reach a first peak in the 1970 Okean exercises, was to be steadily increased until the 1975 Okean exercises and is currently continuing. Later we shall deal with more specific instances of this expansion of the Soviet Navy, moving in the wake of diplomatic incentives, the deployment of economic and military aid detachments, the rejuvenation of fishing capabilities and ports and, finally, the establishment of base facilities. By 1975 the Soviet Navy had reached a strength uncalled for in the protection of a fast-increasing mercantile marine which had no overseas role in war. It included a total of submarines far in excess of those required for home defence and a fleet pattern which made no sense except in the context of world deployment. Admiral Gorshkov's instructions of 1963 to sail out upon the world's oceans, his claim of 1967 that the USSR now possessed "an offensive type of long-range armed force" and his statement of 1973 that "the flag of the Soviet Navy flies over the oceans of the world" need to be taken very seriously in any estimate of the current world situation.

The Soviets Abroad

"Ocean Cruises are a school of moral-political and psychological training for modern war."

"The Soviet Navy is a powerful factor in the creation of favourable conditions for the building of Socialism and Communism, for the active defence of peace and for strengthening international security."

"With the emergence of our ships into the oceans the Navy acquired the capability . . . thoroughly to study the specific features of situations in which it will have to perform its missions in wartime."

In his numerous articles Admiral Gorshkov has provided writers with an unlimited store of quotations but the three above give an accurate summary of the present situation. The Soviet Navy is in a continuing state of training for war at sea and, until such time as it has to use its strength in action, will act as a political force world-wide for the spread of Socialism and Communism. That this last activity looks remarkably like the spread of 19th Century Imperialism is not commented upon by Admiral Gorshkov, nor is the fact that in its exercise a considerable number of bases are being obtained, again very reminiscent of the British coaling-stations so frequently reviled in Soviet writings.

Before the war little was seen of the ships of the Red Fleet beyond its own coastal limits. This was hardly surprising in view of the internal problems in the USSR, a certain lack of professional ability within that fleet and the fact that the USSR had few friends abroad. In 1945, as we have seen in the introduction, the Soviet leaders found their boundaries advanced by many hundreds of miles. Their further expansion into Greece and South Korea was halted but these were land adventures conducted through local national agencies and occurred during the period when the Soviet fleet, although increasing rapidly in size, was still tied to a defensive concept.

Stalin's grandiose schemes for a big-ship fleet capable of operations abroad had been defeated by the war of 1941–45 and it was to take time to resuscitate them. His death in 1953 brought the change of policies already discussed in detail; new plans were afoot but new plans that depend on ships take time to put into effect.

It was about the time of the changeover in the USSR that minor naval deployments took place – none was much more than a port visit except for the group of submarines which was based in Albania in the mid-1950s. This was an ill-starred move as, following the transfer of two "Whisky" class to that country in 1960, the second pair was seized by the Albanians when relations were severed in 1961. Visits to Yugoslavian ports took place during the recurrent periods of semi-amity between the two countries but there was little of significance reported.

By 1958 deployments from the Black Sea, particularly of auxiliaries, was on the increase and lasted for a couple of years, dropping to zero as the Albanian break came. Around the Cuban period of 1962 interest in the Mediterranean was at its lowest level but in 1964 there began a notable increase in the Marmara traffic and the permanent Soviet presence in the Mediterranean was first established. The cause was apparently an upsurge of interest in Turkish-Soviet relationship triggered off by disagreements between Turkey and the USA over Cyprus but, in this case, an easing of the problem did not bring a withdrawal of forces. From 1964 onwards the number of transits through the Turkish Straits increased steadily. In that year some half-dozen ships were normally held in the Mediterranean but, with the Arab-Israeli war of 1967, this figure shot up to seventy. Although reduced at the conclusion of hostilities the Soviet fleet was firmly based in Egypt and it was from Alexandria that most of the forty or so ships permanently established as the Mediterranean squadron were to operate. Large scale exercises took place, assisted by the presence of an average of nine submarines (mainly diesel boats but with some reinforcement of nuclears) from the Northern Fleet and an amphibious group, generally from the Black Sea. AGIs and survey ships operated throughout the area and any Western carriers operating in the Eastern Mediterranean were tailed, normally by warships, frequently missile-armed. Alexandria became a major naval base with a headquarters ashore, communications, docking, refit and repair facilities as well as berths both alongside and at buoys. Further west the port of Mersa Matruh was expanded as a second base and anchorages beyond the three-mile limit were frequently used off Sollum on the Egyptian-Libyan border, Hammamet in Tunisia, Kithera in Southern Greece, off the south coast of Crete and the eastern tip of Cyprus. As time went by Soviet ships also spent prolonged periods in Latakia in Syria whilst Soviet naval aircraft, both *Badger* bombers and reconnaissance planes and A/S amphibians, were stationed at Egyptian bases.

At no time during this period did the Soviet squadron attain numerical superiority over the combined forces of NATO in the Mediterranean – far from it – but when war broke out again between Israel and the Arabs in October 1973 a dramatic reinforcement occurred. From the Black Sea they came and through the Strait of Gibraltar until, in the early days of November, close on 100 ships were gathered. Five cruisers, twenty-two destroyers, frigates and other missile ships, twenty-five submarines, eight landing-ships and craft and thirty-five support ships and AGIs outnumbered the full strength of the US Sixth Fleet. Of course this numerical comparison ignores any qualitative estimate – no fixed-wing aircraft embarked in the Soviet ships who nevertheless had a preponderance in missiles and submarines and all the imponderables of training, command, flexibility – but it does show a tremendous advance in Soviet capability.

But let no-one be deluded by this powerful thrust into the Mediterranean into believing that this is the sole area of expansion – world-wide, Admiral Gorshkov said and world-wide it is. In the Atlantic the submarine patrols continue. "Yankee" class SSBNs off the US Eastern seaboard can, with the 1,600-mile Mod 2 SSN-6, and in conjunction with their sisters on patrol in the Pacific, cover the whole of the USA. Meanwhile the "Delta" class, with 4,200-mile SSN-8 missiles, need not leave the shelter of the Greenland and Norwegian Seas to threaten North America, Europe and a large part of China and her neighbours. Attack submarines deployed into Europe's Western Approaches are in a position not only to gain experience of possible operating areas but to cause disruption and harassment by their very presence if the political situation so requires.

In the Caribbean Soviet infiltration has followed the standard pattern of advice, trade, expansion of embassies and KGB subversion. The first move in maritime expansion is frequently advice and support for local fishing industries and the £15 million Havana fishery centre is typical of such activities. Built in 1962–66 it is provided with facilities for communications, berthing and repair as well as fish-processing for the catches of the 150 or so trawlers which it can accommodate. Although the debacle of October 1962 caused the withdrawal of Soviet missiles it had little long-term impact on the Russians' presence and influence. Soviet research and survey ships continued to operate in the area whilst the Cuban navy was provided with fast attack craft (missile and torpedo) as well as "Kronstadt" and "SO I" class corvettes. By 1969 the situation had reached the stage where Soviet warships could assist matters by a visit and subsequent exercises. On 20 July a "Kynda" class cruiser, a "Kashin" and a "Kildin" class destroyers, two "Foxtrot" submarines, an "Ugra" class support ship and a tanker arrived in Havana. Somewhere in the background was a "November" class nuclear submarine and another tanker. The whole force remained in the area for a month, visiting Martinique and Barbados between exercises, finally departing on 12 August.

In November 1969 Marshal Grechko, the Soviet Defence Minister, visited Cuba, a visit returned in February 1970 by Raul Castro, Minister of the Revolutionary Armed Forces. Soon afterwards the world-wide Soviet naval exercise Okean which took place in April–May 1970 brought a second visit. A "Kresta I", a "Kanin", two "Foxtrots", an "Ugra" and a tanker were joined by an "Echo II" submarine armed with 400-mile

SSN-3 cruise missiles. Not only did this addition up the ante but three pairs of Tu-95 *Bear* bombers visited Cuba on 18 and 25 April and 13 May. The force, which possessed all forms of missile strike ability, air, ship and submarine as well as reconnaissance and mid-course missile guidance by the *Bears*, was a formidable unit which remained in the area from 8 May to 4 June visiting Havana and Cienfuegos.

But the next visit, in September 1970, brought action in its wake. This time the cruiser, destroyer, tanker and submarine-depot ship were joined by an "Alligator" class LST, a buoy tender and a tug, and their visit was centred on Cienfuegos, an almost landlocked harbour in southern Cuba and the site of the Cuban Cayo Loco naval base. The depot-ship secured to buoys, the LST unloaded a pair of barges which had previous submarine associations, booms were set up, and the island of Cayo de Alcatraz blossomed with barracks, sports fields and a water-tower. It looked as though the Soviet Navy had come to stay – a submarine base, if nothing else, on the USA's southern doorstep. On 25 September began a series of exchanges between Washington and Moscow, reminders of the 1962 agreement of "no Soviet missiles in Cuba equals no US invasion", denials by the USSR that there was any base in prospect in Cuba, arguments about the servicing of Soviet nuclear submarines in or around Cuba. The upshot was that on 8 January 1971 the depot-ship left the area, having transferred from Cienfuegos to Mariel in October. Whilst this diplomatic activity continued another squadron of a destroyer, a "Foxtrot" and a tanker visited Cuba in November 1970 leaving at the same time as the depot-ship, presumably to prove that the Soviets were neither dismayed nor deterred by the US action. More visits were to follow in February–March 1971, May–June 1971, October 1971–January 1972, March–May 1972, November 1972–February 1973, August 1973, April–May 1974, September 1974, February–March 1975 and during Exercise Okean 75. In nearly all these fourteen cases (bar four, possibly) at least one submarine was included in the visiting squadron.

In the Eastern Atlantic a permanent presence was established rather later than in the Caribbean. In the wake of the Portuguese-supported invasion of Guinea in November 1970 two Soviet destroyers appeared off Conakry to provide support for President Sekou Touré. Although these spent the majority of their time at sea, later visits have been to the harbour at Conakry and have included not only the permanent patrols but also ships on passage to and from the East and an LST loaded with military stores. At the airfield Tu-95 *Bear* bombers have paid frequent visits and from here flew a series of sorties in support of Okean 75.

Almost due East from Conakry, some 3,500 miles away on the East coast of Africa, lies the Somali port of Berbera. Here a major fishing facility was constructed by the Soviets in the 1960s – aid to the backward Somalis. Go-downs, berthing, refrigerated stores, cranes were all provided. It was, therefore, no surprise that the first Soviet deployment to the Indian Ocean in March–July 1968 did not visit Berbera – they knew the place. The timing of this cruise is interesting. The British, intent upon a policy of dismembering what remained of their Imperial connections, had pulled out of the Indian Ocean (except for a peripheral presence in the Gulf and off Beira and Singapore) in November–December 1967. Admiral Gorshkov visited India in February 1968 and, on 27 March, a not unimpressive squadron of a "Sverdlov" with two destroyers and tankers entered Madras. From then on it was Bombay, Mogadishu, Umm Quasr, Karachi, Bandar Abbas at the same time as Marshal Zakharov, Chief of the General Staff was present, Berenice in Egypt, Aden and

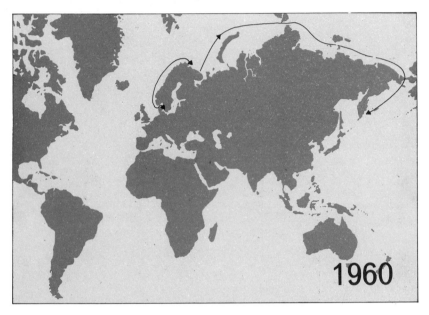

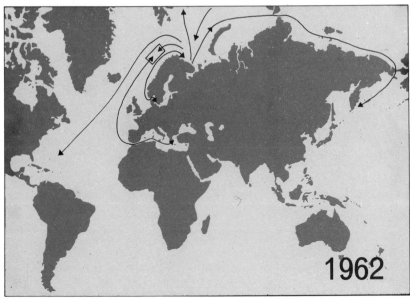

Colombo and so back home to Vladivostok. It was an impressive performance – eight countries in four months, between four and eight days in each place – and made clear the fact that the new-Imperialists had learned a major lesson.

Later in the year, from November 1968 to 1 May 1969, came the second round of visits, this time by a combined squadron from the Pacific, Northern and Black Sea Fleets which, for the first time, included two submarines. It was Mombasa, Aden, Massawa, Hodeida, Bandar Abbas, Umm Quasr, Dar-es-Salaam, Chittagong and Mauritius which now

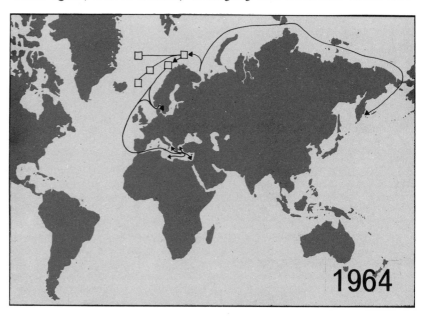

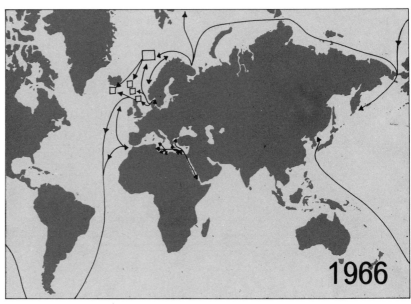

received attention – five more countries in the bag. Barely had this party dispersed when a "Krupny" with her tanker from the Pacific sailed to Umm Quasr, Bandar Abbass, Zanzibar and Male in the Maldives. Only one new state was included in this cruise which lasted from May to October 1969 and overlapped with the next party which broke new ground in that it contained an "Alligator" LST and visited a new country, Sudan.

One can go on with lists of ships and ports and dates until the reader becomes jaded. The important points are these:

(a) Since 1969 all the countries with a seaboard on the Indian Ocean,

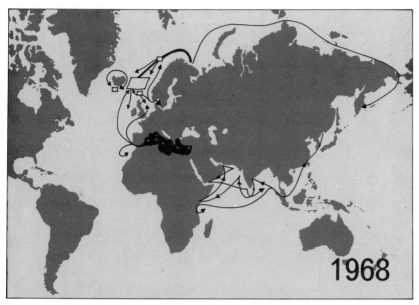

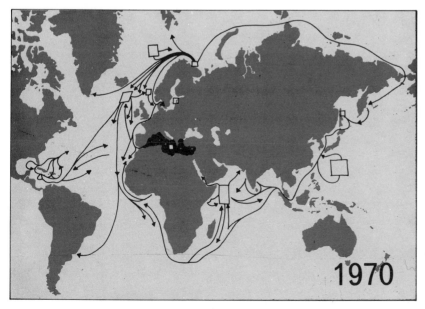

Red Sea and Persian Gulf from Tanzania to Bangladesh excepting Saudi Arabia, Oman, the United Arab Emirates, Qatar, Bahrain and Kuwait have received frequent and sometimes prolonged visits from Soviet naval units.

(b) These forces have included elements of nearly every major modern class of ship and submarine – presumably a long-term study of environmental problems.

(c) Since the initial Grand Tours the main Soviet interest in the Indian Ocean has been centred on the Arabian Sea/Red Sea area.

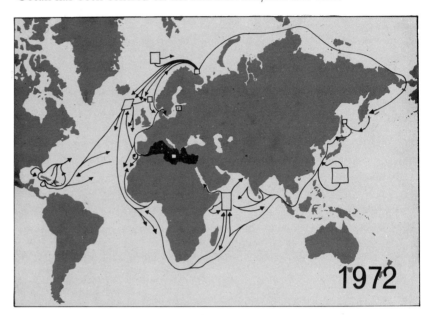

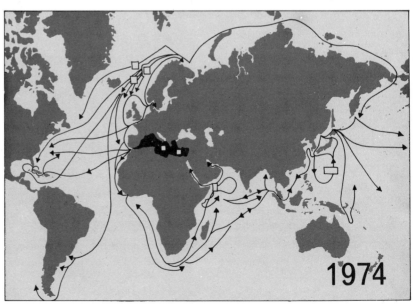

(d) Anchorages have been established on the perimeter of this area in International waters in the Chagos Archipelago, the Seychelles and off Socotra.

(e) A base with repair, refuelling, communications and missile facilities has been established at Berbera, whence Soviet naval aircraft also operate.

(f) A weekly *Aeroflot* flight visits Mauritius to bring spare crews to the Soviet trawlers in the area.

(g) Frequent refuelling visits are made to Aden.

(h) The opening of the Suez Canal has lessened the distance from the Black Sea to Berbera from about 7,000 miles round the Cape of Good Hope to barely 2,000.

The last major area of deployment is the Pacific Ocean and it is here that the least increase has been observed over the past fifteen years, although many ships have passed through it on passage to other localities. Apart from the deployment of SSBNs to the west coast of the USA, considerable activity by research and survey ships and the deployment of vessels during a missile firing into the sea, the majority of Pacific Fleet activity has remained "in area". This is not really surprising as a large part of the eastern seaboard of the Pacific is controlled by Canada and the USA, and the latter has made her feelings clear over any interference in North or South America. With the Western seaboard made up of the inhospitable coasts of China, Japan and Indonesia, with US interest in the Philippines and little to be gained in Australasia the sole remaining area to be probed is the tumultuous area of South East Asia. Here the possibility of active involvement has probably been too high during the recent wars and it may be that the very independent groups of Communists now in control have made their determination to remain independent quite clear. Overtures to Singapore have been made through the medium of merchant ship repair requests but one cannot see this becoming much more than a business relationship while Lee Kuan Yew is in charge.

The maps on the preceding pages show more clearly than any words what has happened over the last fifteen years. As other navies have retreated so has that of the Soviets moved outwards including in their development the two very large world-wide naval exercises Okean 1970 and 1975 involving 200–220 ships and submarines. Today, they are a deep-water navy well provided with ships, experienced in operations world-wide, well placed to redeploy as situations are created and well supported by a growing force of naval supply ships and the most numerous merchant navy in the world.

SOVIET NAVAL BASES

Northern Fleet

Severomorsk — Ice-free fleet base in the Kola Inlet. Headquarters of C-in-C Northern Fleet.

Polyarny — Submarine base in the Kola Inlet.

Baltic Fleet

Leningrad — Shipyards only with numerous naval training establishments.

Kronstadt — On eastern end of Kotlin Island. Naval base with repair facilities.

Tallin — Generally ice-free port and naval base for smaller classes of ships.

Liepaja — Naval base and repair facilities. Submarine base.

Kaliningrad — Naval base. Headquarters Soviet Naval Air Force (Baltic).

Baltiisk — Headquarters of C-in-C Baltic Fleet. Naval Air Station in vicinity. Base for destroyers, submarines, fast attack craft and KGB Border Guards.

Black Sea Fleet

Sevastopol — Fleet base with repair facilities on south of Crimean Peninsula. Headquarters of C-in-C Black Sea Fleet. Submarine base at Balaclava.

Novorossisk — Base for Light Forces to east of Straits of Kerch.

Tuapse — South-east of Novorossisk. Minor naval base.

Poti — South-east of Tuapse. Minor naval base.

Batumi — Close to Turkish border. Minor naval base.

Odessa — Minor naval base.

Sochi — Minor naval base.

Caspian Flotilla

Baku 100 miles from Iranian border. Minor naval base. Headquarters Caspian Flotilla.

Pacific Fleet

Vladivostok At southern end of Muraiev Peninsula and close to mouth of Ussuri River and within 100 miles of Chinese and North Korean borders. Headquarters of C-in-C Pacific Fleet. Main Fleet base with large submarine school and building yards.

Sovetskaya Gavan 300 miles east of Khabarovsk on the coast inside Sakhalin. Base for submarines, destroyers and below. Building and repair facilities, and submarine school.

Korsakov At southern end of Sakhalin. Minor naval base with air station.

Petropavlovsk On south-east coast of Kamchatka Peninsula. Major naval base. Number of naval air stations in area.

Magadan Minor naval base on northern shore of Sea of Okhotsk for summer use only.

Note: As well as the above bases there are numerous commercial ports with facilities available for naval purposes.

Command Structure

In common with all activities in the USSR the organisation of the Soviet Navy is eventually controlled by the Central Committee CPSU, their instructions being transmitted through and by the Minister of Defence, currently Marshal Grechko, a member of the Politburo and Defence Council. He is backed by three first-deputy- and nine deputy-ministers, amongst these being the chiefs of the armed forces, and served by the unified General Staff on which there is always a very senior Naval officer, currently Admiral-of-the-Fleet S. M. Lobov. The subsequent steps in the organisational ladder date from the period in 1953 immediately following upon the death of Stalin. At the head of naval affairs and in a position comparable to an amalgamation of that of the British First Sea Lord and the old British appointment of First Lord of the Admiralty, is the Commander-in-Chief, Soviet Navy, a position held since 5 January 1956 by Admiral-of-the-Fleet of the Soviet Union Sergei Gorshkov. Both the man and the rank are unique, for it is his vision, ability and maintenance of control which have been the main forces behind the build-up of the present fleet. His immediate assistant in this task is the First Deputy C-in-C who, as well as having four (possibly five) Deputy Cs-in-C (two of whom are Engineer officers), has the Chief of the Main Naval Staff, the Chief of the Political Directorate and the Naval Council (Soviet), a senior consultative group of some eleven members, under his charge. The Political Directorate, whose chief is a member of the Naval Council, also has a responsibility to the Main Political Administration of the Armed Forces and thence upwards to the Central Committee, an additional line of authority which was first forged in 1921. In addition to this group of senior officers and the First Deputy Chief of Naval Staff are the Chiefs of the more specialised departments – Naval Aviation (the only Type Commander in the organisation), Naval Infantry, Personnel, Coast Defence, Training, Intelligence, Security, the Hydrographic Service and Naval Law. The Chief of Rear Services (logistics), is also to be included here but may, in fact, be the fifth Deputy C-in-C.

The Soviet Navy, whose relations with its commissars has not always been of the best, now relies on the Political Directorate for political training as well as welfare. Officers of this branch are no longer solely responsible for non-operational matters – they can be eligible not only for watch-keeping but also for command.

The organisation of the fleets themselves reflect the senior command structure. With a C-in-C, First Deputy C-in-C, Chief of Staff and Head of the Political Directorate the responsibility is vested in them for not only the sea-going ships and submarine operations (possibly excluding the SSBNs) but also for the Naval Infantry, shore support and bases, Naval Aviation, coast-defence forces, hydrographic and meteorological services, dockyards, training establishments and Rear Services (logistics). The fleets are thus almost totally self-contained units, a necessity when one considers the vast distances and geographical separation involved. This does not mean, however, that the central command cannot and does not exercise control over their movements and operations. The two Okean exercises in 1970 and 1975 demonstrated very clearly a highly efficient command and communications system capable of coordinating actions world-wide. Failures in this direction are more likely to be at the operator's end than at Headquarters.

Of the six satellite countries remaining in the Warsaw Pact after Albania's withdrawal in 1968 in protest against the invasion of Czechoslovakia only two have fleets of any proportions, East Germany and Poland. Hungary and Czechoslovakia have river patrol forces and Bulgaria and Romania small naval forces. Until recently the latter have consisted almost entirely of Soviet-built ships – in 1974, however, Romania displayed a new force of Chinese-designed "Shanghai" class fast attack craft and a "Hu Chwan" hydrofoil.

The East Germans' main strength lies in light forces and minesweepers while the Poles, with an excellent record in submarine operations in the Second World War, operate four "Whisky" class boats in addition to a powerful amphibious group, light forces, minesweepers and a naval air force. Both navies normally participate in Baltic exercises at the same time as major Soviet exercises take place further afield. There is little doubt that there is close coordination of all these forces by the Moscow centre, although from time to time they carry out independent exercises off their own coasts.

Command Structure

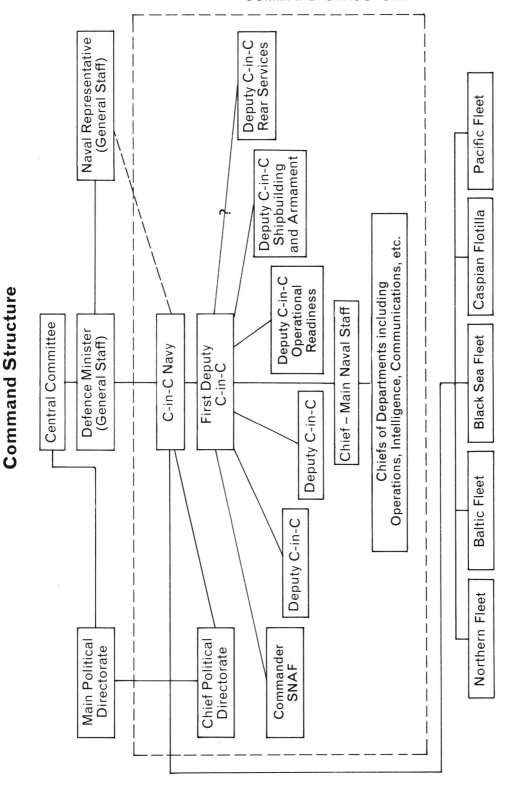

COMMAND STRUCTURE

Central Committee

Defence Minister (General Staff)

Naval Representative (General Staff)

Deputy C-in-C Rear Services

Deputy C-in-C Shipbuilding and Armament

Deputy C-in-C Operational Readiness

C-in-C Navy

First Deputy C-in-C

Deputy C-in-C

Chief – Main Naval Staff

Chiefs of Departments including Operations, Intelligence, Communications, etc.

Main Political Directorate

Chief Political Directorate

Commander SNAF

Northern Fleet

Baltic Fleet

Black Sea Fleet

Caspian Flotilla

Pacific Fleet

Manpower and Training

With a strength of about half a million officers and men the Soviet Navy is faced with continual problems of training and transition. Whilst the officers are both volunteers and long-service professionals some 70 per cent of the navy consists of conscripts serving for three years if afloat and two years if shore based. This reversal of what would be the more likely solution in Western navies suggests two things – an effort to reduce inevitable turbulence in sea-going appointments and the fact that such appointments are preferable to duty ashore.

The officers of this largely conscript-manned fleet require a high degree of technical knowledge if maintenance of increasingly complex ships is to be kept at an acceptable level. There is certainly no lack of volunteers and these, on selection, are given a five-year training period ashore, a large proportion of this time being occupied with theoretical technical instruction. This is carried out at eleven establishments – five at Leningrad, Kaliningrad, Sevastopol, Baku and Vladivostock for general service officers, of whom some become submariners, one at Leningrad for submariners, one at Pushkin, near Leningrad for radar and sonar, three at Leningrad and Sevastopol for engineers and one at Kiev for political officers, who do only four years' instruction. Straightaway one is struck by the very early separation of the cadets into their eventual specialisations, giving little chance of any exchange of ideas with those who will eventually work with them in their ships. The second notable point is the extremely long period which exists between new entry and a sea-going appointment; a defect which is now being remedied to some degree by the use of training ships such as the two "Ugras" and the older cruisers.

The training given during these five years is apparently of an improved standard with more up-to-date training aids although instruction in the fundamentals of naval operations remains fairly elementary. The emphasis on technical matters is shown by the fact that all officer graduates, except those from the political school, receive engineering diplomas. Naval Air Force cadets, four years of whose training is carried out by the Air Force, are given one year's instruction in naval matters at a special school. With the introduction of the new "Kuril" class carriers it seems possible that a longer period of naval instruction for those who will pilot the embarked aircraft may be necessary but the very compartmented approach adopted in the Soviet Navy may rule against this.

The main weight of an officer's training is therefore concentrated in his initial period in the navy, a plan which is very different from that current in Western navies. However, there are later opportunities for sub-specialisation courses, some lasting as long as two years. But the divisive pattern is set in the formative years and, although undesirable, is probably inevitable.

The first occasion when some officers are given the opportunity to broaden their outlook is when, and if, they are selected to attend the Order of Lenin Naval Academy in Leningrad. Although this single establishment cannot meet the ever-increasing need for officers with a broader and more educated background it is a highly efficient staff college with modern ideas and equipment. Its graduates are well trained and from their ranks come the senior officers of later years.

The junior officers in a ship retain the highly specialised approach inculcated in the various schools and, to ensure continuity in a fleet deficient in skilled ratings and to provide a backing of technical ability, they remain for long periods in the same ship. This may extend to a steady increase in responsibility culminating, in some cases, in command of the ship which he joined from new-entry training. This is not quite so astonishing as it seems because a number of young officers aged around 28–30 are these days appointed in command of certain of the newer destroyers. Command of the more important ships is, however, reserved for senior captains whilst a fairly high proportion of both ballistic-missile and fleet submarines are, similarly, commanded by Captain 1st rank.

The main theme throughout is concentration on technical ability and the reason for this becomes clear when the rating structure is considered. By the Military Service Law of 1 January 1968 the length of service afloat was cut from four years to three and the call-up age was reduced to 18. In one move the Soviet authorities had ensured a greater reservoir of reservists at the expense of manning the fleet with a higher proportion of callow, if malleable, youths and decreasing the time in which the Navy is able to capitalise on their training. Admittedly the conscript will have undergone pre-entry tuition in a factory, school or collective farm but, with a generally lower standard of intellect than his average Western counterpart, it is hardly surprising that his training and subsequent employment is confined by narrow limits. The overall training programme for the conscripts is an enormous task for the authorities as the biannual intake in the spring and autumn of each year is about 60,000. Before going to his first ship the conscript receives six months' intensive tuition in the specialised subject chosen for him and joins as a junior seaman. In this position he receives payment of approximately £3 per month, compared with the average Soviet worker's income of £50 per month. But he is young, has no food or lodging to pay for, no family to support, no gambling or drinking and no opportunity to spend his few roubles during foreign visits. He knows that if he is diligent he can, if chosen for advancement to a more senior rate, achieve a pay of about £40 a month at the end of his three years' conscript service. Throughout this time he will have toiled for longer hours than most other navies' ratings, will have been carefully nurtured in the doctrine of state Communism, and, should he show the necessary aptitude, have been cross-trained with another specialisation during his third year. It is difficult to see how this plan can promote efficiency although it most certainly appears to be a factor in reducing the size of ships' companies. The emphasis on a narrow-based user/maintainer approach, the policy of repair by replacement and the increasing reliance on base rather than underway maintenance are all probably part of an attempt to alleviate the problems caused by a serious lack of trained senior ratings.

By the end of his conscription the bright young man of 21 can have been rated a Petty Officer First Class. The great majority of ratings prefer to opt out at the end of their three years but those who volunteer for a further stint will amost invariably be rated Chief Petty Officer. By 1971 the response to the call to re-enlist was so poor that a new rate, that of Michman, equivalent in many ways except experience, ability and age to the British Fleet Chief, was introduced. This rate carried greater privileges and pay as well as a chance of eventual promotion to officer. It superseded all other forms of re-engagement, required a longer term of commitment and was, apparently, as unpopular as the previous arrangements which have subsequently been reintroduced.

The need for a narrow and specialised training imposed by a wholly conscript junior rating structure has brought other and more fundamental problems in its wake. With little experience amongst the majority of the inadequate force of senior ratings they are allowed little initiative in their duties. This is a basic failing at all levels in a navy where centralised control is much practised and where there is a most undemocratic adherence to the rule of rank which frequently results in senior officers taking charge over their juniors' heads in a manner alien to Western methods.

From the foregoing emerges a picture in which very complex ships are manned by officers with an advanced technical background who remain with their ships for long periods. The lack of skilled ratings, both senior and junior, must mean that a deal of extra work and responsibility devolves upon the junior officer, particularly when one realises that ships' companies are less numerous than in Western navies. This may be due to an emphasis on shore-based maintenance, a measure of cross-specialisation amongst the senior conscripts and, possibly, an administrative decision to impose a manning standard adequate for peace-time operations and sufficient to take part in a brief "one-shot" war should deterrence fail.

The morale of these ships' companies is very largely in the hands of the political officers and indoctrination in party matters probably assists in providing a sense of purpose and a cohesion between ethnic groups which would otherwise be lacking. As some 70 % of the officers are Communist Party members those presumably make their contribution to the political aspect of affairs. How many of them are true believers and what number scent promotional advantage it is impossible to say but one thing that is certain is that a large proportion of the junior officers has been raised in an atmosphere of "getting to sea" and this, irrespective of political motivation, must have a beneficial effect on morale. Even though only some 8–10% of the total numbers of ships and submarines available are deployed "out-of-area" (ie beyond the limits of local areas) the resultant improvement in spirit is clear.

A frequent query is "How do the Soviet sailors stand up to such deployments?" Their ships are provided with accommodation of an austerity unknown in Western navies, cramped and over-crowded. Airconditioning is normally confined to operational spaces, although the latest classes may show some improvement in this respect. Victualling is also poor by Western standards but in all these matters it must be remembered that conditions of both board and lodging in the Soviet Union are generally much lower than in the effete democracies. Under these conditions, however, lengthy deployments in tropical conditions could well result in medical problems, although any sailors who are landed during port visits appear fit and healthy. There is no way of judging the condition of those who remain on board.

Nor, to be totally objective, is there any means of judging the condition of the navy as a whole. Available evidence suggests that no more than a mediocre standard of maintenance can be achieved and yet these ships remain on foreign deployments for long periods. During these periods they apparently suffer little from engineering defects, they are rarely involved in collisions and groundings and the majority of their radars and sonars appear to function satisfactorily. Whether their missiles and guns can be fired is never demonstrated out-of-area. A purely personal impression is that this is a fleet where, by the technical competence of the officers, simple and rugged design of machinery, an excellent shore-based maintenance organisation and an adequate complement of carried-onboard spares, a small proportion of the ships is maintained at sea for lengthy periods. That this proportion is a lot lower than in Western navies may be an act of policy or may be due to inadequacies in ships' companies. The final impression is that the Soviet Navy might well be hard-pushed to sustain a long-term conventional war.

Insignia of Rank

Junior Lieutenant
Mladshiy Leytenant

Lieutenant *Leytenant*

Senior Lieutenant
Starshiy Leytenant

Captain Lieutenant
Kapitan Leytenant

Captain Third Rank
Kapitan Tretyego Ranga

Captain Second Rank
Kapitan Vtorogo Ranga

Captain First Rank
Kapitan Pervogo Ranga

Rear Admiral
Kontr-Admiral

Vice Admiral
Vitse-Admiral

Admiral *Admiral*

Fleet Admiral
Admiral Flota

Fleet Admiral of the
Soviet Union
*Admiral Flota
Sovetskgogo Soyuza*

Soviet Shipbuilding

At the end of the Great Patriotic War in 1945 the Soviet shipyards in the west were mostly in ruins. At the start of hostilities in 1941 what existed was inadequate for the massive naval building programme announced under the Third Five Year Plan (1938–43). This lack had been noted by the Eighteenth Communist Party Conference in 1939, underlined by the C-in-C Navy in the following year and was still existing at the time of the German invasion. With surface-ship building concentrated at the Admiralty and Ordzhonikidze Yards at Leningrad and the two major yards at Nikolayev it was not to be long before these were invested or over-run by the enemy. Nine other yards were under construction at this time, the main emphasis being on the submarine slips at Gorky, on the Volga some 300 miles East from Moscow, a second major submarine centre at the Molotovsk Yard at Archangel and the Komsomolsk Yard on the Amur River in the East. This wide distribution of shipbuilding facilities away from the main battlefronts enabled construction to continue during the war, although it was chiefly confined to submarines and minor vessels.

Thus by 1945 it was this form of shipbuilding which was all that remained and if Stalin's call in July 1945 for a powerful navy was to be followed a vast rehabilitation task was needed. This was soon under way and, in the next five years, resulted in the delivery of five cruisers and fifteen destroyers. Nor was this effort at the expense of the number of submarines completed. A steady delivery rate of "Shch", "Stalinets" and "Malutka" class boats was soon followed by the astonishing acceleration of "Whisky" class programme which produced 240 submarines between 1951 and 1957. Alongside this ran the "Zulu" programme of twenty-five boats and the twenty-two "Quebec" class, incorporating an HTP turbine for high-speed work. These figures are quoted to give some idea of the immense capacity for production in a country which had just endured the destruction of a third of its economy and while Great Britain was still under intensified rationing and the Marshall Plan was enabling the Western European countries to find their economic feet.

By the mid-1950s the pattern of Soviet naval construction had reached a general layout similar to that which exists today (1975).

In the north, at Archangel, the Molotovsk Yard had been renamed Severodvinsk. Here, on an increasingly large complex of covered ways, work was concentrated on submarines. From here came the first nuclear-propelled submarines, the "November" class, in 1959. Subsequently the "Hotel" class of SSBNs was to be followed by the "Yankees", and this cold, inhospitable area had become the largest submarine building centre in the world.

With the wisdom of dispersion apparent from their recent experiences, the USSR installed their second nuclear submarine building facility at Komsomolsk, some 300 miles from the Pacific on the Amur River. Here the first of the "Echo" class cruise-missile boats were constructed, to be followed later by "Yankee" class SSBNs. In 1968 the lead boats of the new generation of cruise-missile nuclear submarines, the "Charlie" class, were completed at Gorky, thus continuing the long association of this yard with submarines, although it is also a centre for mercantile construction as well as ships for the inland waterways and hydrofoils. Other submarine yards are now situated at Leningrad (Sudomekh and Admiralty Yards).

The main centres for surface-ship building remain Leningrad (Zhdanov), Kaliningrad, Nikolayev (North and South), Kamysh Buruu (Kerch) and Khabarovsk. The first of these has a long record of cruiser and destroyer construction. Nikolayev (South) has been the home of the newer classes of big ships and from here have come the helicopter cruisers of the "Moskva" class, and the "Kuril" class aircraft carriers. Nikolayev (North) has been primarily occupied with the "Kara" class cruisers, destroyers and smaller types whilst Khabarovsk is a centre for the building of destroyers and below.

In addition to the building yards in the Soviet Union both East Germany and Poland produce a large proportion of the survey and research ships, amphibious vessels and tugs used by the Soviet Navy. The main German yards are at Wismar, Rostock, Warnemünde, Peene/Wolgast and Stralsund, although the last is mainly concerned with the production of fishing vessels. Poland's shipbuilding is centred on Gdansk, Gdynia and Szczecin.

It is clear from the foregoing that the Soviet High Command has a very large shipyard capacity available and it should be remembered that, from the naval point of view, this is by no means fully extended by current (1975) construction programmes, although conversions, refits and maintenance must occupy a large part of this capacity. The geographical position of many of the yards has required exceptional arrangements to overcome the extreme climatic conditions. Heated and covered slipways and covered-in floating docks are only some of these additions which, combined with designers whose efficiency is increased by long-term tenure of office and a closely-integrated and apparently enthusiastic labour-force are ensuring a steady output of efficient and well-built ships.

SOVIET NAVAL SHIPYARDS

Name	Position	Coordinates North East	Type of Construction	Capacity	Notes
Severodvinsk (ex-Molotovsk)	30 miles North-West of Archangel	64.27 39.58	Primarily submarines	Up to 6 slips all covered and heated	Completed late 1930s
Leningrad – Admiralty (ex-Marti, ex-Purilov)	On Galerny Is.		Primarily submarines	1 major and 3 minor slips, 2 Fitting-out basins	Completed 1900
Zhdanov	Near Leningrad Commercial Port	All within a few miles of 59.55 30.20	Cruisers and destroyers	5 slips up to 600 ft	Completed late 1930s. Building yard for hulls – fitting out at other yards
Sudomekh	Inside Vasilevsky Is. on R. Neva		Destroyers and below, Submarines	1 750-ft slip, 3 400-ft slips	Completed lated 1930s
Baltic (ex-Ordzhonikidze)	On Vasilevsky Is. at mouth of R. Neva		Destroyers, Cruisers, Submarines, Auxiliaries	3 large slips up to 900 ft. Two 5-ship beam-on slips. Dry dock. Covered building slip	Completed mid-19th Century
Petrovsky	On Petrovsky Is.		Minor warships	Small slips	Completed late 1930s
Tallinn	Opposite Helsinki	59.29 24.58	Destroyers and below, possibly submarines	Seven slips, two dry docks	Originally as Revel Yard belonged to Nobel (Sweden). Derelict for 30 years until rebuilt 1945
Liepaja	On Latvian Coast, East of Öland	56.30 21.00	Minesweepers and minor craft	Two dry docks. Several small slips	Post-war development
Klaipeda	On Lithuanian Coast 60 miles South of Liepaja	55.43 21.10	Minesweepers and minor craft	Several small slips	Ex-German Lindenau Yard
Kaliningrad (ex-Königsberg)	East of Baltijsk (ex-Pillau)	54.42 20.32	Destroyers and below	Several small slips	Ex-German Schichau Yard

Name	Position	Coordinates		Type of Construction	Capacity	Notes
		North	East			
Gorky	300 miles East of Moscow on R. Volga	56.20	44.00	Submarines and minor war vessels	Several slips up to 400 ft	Completed late 1930s
Zelendolsk	150 miles East of Gorky on R. Volga	55.55	48.30	Minor war vessels	—	Post war completion
Nikolaev – Nosenko, North and South Yards.	70 miles North-East of Odessa on R. Bug	46.58	32.07	South Yard – aircraft-carriers, helicopter-cruisers, cruisers. North Yard – cruisers and below, submarines	Two 1,000-ft slips. 15 other slips from 800 ft down. 50,000-ton floating dock	19th Century yards – North Yard being the oldest of existing Russian shipyards (c 1800 – rebuilt after the war)
Kerch (Kamysh Burun)	At entrance to Sea of Azov	45.20	36.20	Destroyers and below	—	—
Komsomolsk	300 miles up R. Amur	50.30	137.00	Submarines, destroyers and below	Several sizeable slips	Completed late 1930s. Fitting out of large ships takes place in Vladivostok due to shallow water at river mouth
Khabarovsk	150 miles above Komsomolsk on R. Amur	48.20	135.00	Frigates and below	—	Completed post-war
Sovetskaya Gavan	On coast inside Sakhalin	48.50	140.00	Destroyers and below	—	Recently completed. Primarily a naval base
Vladivostok	Close to mouth of R. Ussuri on Muraiev Peninsula	43.10	131.53	Destroyers and below and conversions	Several slips	Main fleet base

Note:
(a) Merchant ship construction takes place in addition to naval building at Leningrad (Zhdanov, Admiralty and Baltic), Klaipeda, Kaliningrad, Gorky, Zelenodolsk, Nikolaev (North and South), Kerch and Komsomolsk.
(b) Merchant ship construction only takes place at Vyborg, Kherson and Oktyabrskoye.
(c) The total number of Soviet shipyards represents approximately 20% of the world's major yards. In yards capable of nuclear submarine construction the USSR owns five – the rest, five.

PART II

Flag Officers, Soviet Navy

Commander-in-Chief of the Soviet Navy and First Deputy Ministry of Defence:
  Admiral of the Fleet of the Soviet Union Sergei Georgiyevich Gorshkov
First Deputy Commander-in-Chief of the Soviet Navy: Admiral of the Fleet
  N. I. Smirnov
Assistant Chief of the General Staff of the Armed Forces: Admiral of the Fleet
  S. M. Lobov
Deputy Commander-in-Chief: Admiral N. N. Amelko
Deputy Commander-in-Chief: Engineer Admiral P. G. Kotov
Deputy Commander-in-Chief: Engineer Vice-Admiral V. G. Novikov
Deputy Commander-in-Chief: Admiral G. A. Bondarenko
Commander of Naval Aviation: Colonel-General A. A. Mironenko
Chief of Political Directorate: Admiral V. M. Grishanov
Chief of Rear Services: Vice-Admiral L. Y. Mizin
Chief of Naval Training Establishments: Vice-Admiral I. M. Kuznetsov
Chief of Main Naval Staff: Admiral of the Fleet N. D. Sergeyev
1st Deputy Chief of the Main Naval Staff: Admiral V. N. Alekseyev
Chief of the Hydrographic Service: Admiral A. I. Rassokho

Northern Fleet

Commander-in-Chief: Admiral of the Fleet G. M. Yegorov
1st Deputy Commander-in-Chief: Vice-Admiral Ye. I. Volobuyev
Chief of Staff: Vice-Admiral V. G. Kichev
In Command of the Political Department: Vice-Admiral A. I. Sorokin

Pacific

Commander-in-Chief: Vice-Admiral V. P. Maslov
1st Deputy Commander-in-Chief: —
Chief of Staff: Vice-Admiral V. V. Sidorov
In Command of the Political Department: Vice-Admiral S. S. Bevz

Black Sea

Commander-in-Chief: Vice-Admiral N. I. Khovrin
1st Deputy Commander-in-Chief: Vice-Admiral V. Samoylov
Chief of Staff: Rear-Admiral V. Kh. Saakyan
In Command of the Political Department: Rear-Admiral P. Medvedev

Baltic

Commander-in-Chief: Admiral V. V. Mikhailin
1st Deputy Commander-in-Chief: Rear Admiral Ya. M. Kudelkin
Chief of Staff: Vice-Admiral A. Kosov
In Command of the Political Department: Vice-Admiral N. I. Shablikov

Caspian Flotilla

Commander-in-Chief: Rear Admiral L. D. Ryabtsev
In Command of the Political Department: Rear-Admiral V. N. Sergeyev

Leningrad Naval Base

Commanding Officer: Vice-Admiral V. M. Leonenkov
In Command of the Political Department: Rear-Admiral A. A. Plekhanov
Head of the Order of Lenin Naval Academy: Admiral V. S. Sysoyev
Head of Frunze Naval College: Vice-Admiral V. A. Khrenov

Soviet Naval Strengths

Class	North	Baltic	Black Sea & Caspian	Pacific	Total
Submarines					
Delta II	1	—	—	—	1
Delta	14	—	—	—	14
Yankee	26	—	—	8	34
Hotel III	1	—	—	—	1
Hotel II	5	—	—	3	8
Papa	1	—	—	—	1
Charlie	12	—	—	—	12
Echo II	15	—	—	12	27
Echo I	1	—	—	—	1
Uniform	1	—	—	—	1
November	9	—	—	4	13
Victor	14	—	—	2	16
Golf I & II	14	—	—	8	22
Zulu V	1	—	—	—	1
Juliet	11	—	—	5	16
W Twin Cylinder	5	2	1	4	5
W Long Bin					7
Alpha	1	—	—	—	1
Bravo	1	1	1	1	4
Tango	—	—	3	—	3
Foxtrot	31	14	—	11	56
Romeo	—	5	9	—	14
Quebec	—	11	11	—	22
Zulu IV	9	3	3	4	19
Whisky	10	40	22	28	100
Whisky Canvas Bag	1	—	—	2	3
Surface Ships					
Kuril	—	—	1 + 1	—	1 + 1
Kara	1	—	2	—	3
Moskva	—	—	2	—	2
Sverdlov	2	3	4	3	12

THE SOVIET NAVY TODAY

Class	North	Baltic	Black Sea & Caspian	Pacific	Total
Chapaev	1	1	—	—	2
Kresta II	3	2	1	—	6 + 2
Kresta I	3	—	—	1	4
Kynda	—	—	2	2	4
Krivak	1	6	2	—	9
Kashin	3	3	8	5	19
Kanin	3	2	—	1	6
Krupny	—	—	—	1	1
SAM Kotlin	2	1	3	2	8
Kildin	—	2	2	—	4
Kotlin	3	3	4	8	18
Tallin	—	1	—	—	1
Skory	10	10	10	10	40
Nanuchka	3	5	4	—	12
Mirka I and II	4	4	8	4	20
Petya I and II	10	12	13	10	45
Kola	—	1	3	2	6
Riga	10	9	12	9	40
Ugra	5	3	—	2	10
Lama	2	—	1	2	5
Don	3	—	—	3	6
Grisha	4	6	5	2	17
Poti	25	25	5	15	70
Kronstadt	5	4	4	4	17
Purga	—	1	—	—	1
Amga	1	—	—	—	1
Alesha	1	1	—	—	2
W. Bauer	1	1	—	—	2
Amur	4	4	—	4	12
Oskol	3	3	1	3	10
Atrek	4	1	—	1	6
Dnepr	4	1	—	—	5
Tovda	—	1	—	—	1
Fleet Sweepers	40	61	40	50	191 (16 Natya 45 Yurka 20 T 58 110 T 43)
Coastal Sweepers	25	46	25	25	121 (3 Sonya 3 Zhenya 70 Vanya 40 Sasha 5 T 301)
Inshore Sweepers	25	25	25	25	100
Pchela	—	10	15	—	25

SOVIET NAVAL STRENGTHS

Class	North	Baltic	Black Sea & Caspian	Pacific	Total
Turya	—	6	6	—	12
Komar	—	5	10	—	15
Osa	25	35	25	35	120 (65 Type I 55 Type II)
Stenka	10	24	4	7	45
SO 1	—	40	30	10	80
MO VI	—	15	—	—	15
FAC – Torpedo	15	60	15	40	130 (45 Shershen 80 P6, 8, 10 5 P4)
River Patrol Craft	—	10	40	40	90 (40 Schmel 30 BK III 20 BKL IV)
Alligator	2	4	3	3	12
Polnocny	12	15	18	15	60
Landing Craft	15	16	30	20	81 (10 MP 10 5 MP 8 8 MP 6 15 MP 4 8 MP 2 35 Vydra)
Intelligence Ships (AGIs)	16	8	15	15	54

Overall Totals

(Figures in italics indicate ships being built and are approximate)

Aircraft Carriers	1 + *1*	Frigates	111
Helicopter Cruisers	2	Corvettes (Missile)	26 + *2*
Submarines (SSBN)	58 + *10*	Corvettes	170
Submarines (SSB)	23	Fast Attack Craft (Missile)	135
Submarines (SSGN)	40		
Submarines (SSG)	28	Fast Attack Craft (Patrol)	60
Submarines (SSN)	32 + *3*		
Submarines (SS)	221	Fast Attack Craft (Hydrofoil)	37 + *3*
Cruisers (CLG)	20 + *2*		
Cruisers (Gun)	11	Fast Attack Craft (Torpedo)	125
Destroyers (DDG)	47 + *2*		
Destroyers (Gun)	59	River Patrol Craft	90

Minesweepers – Ocean	191	Space Associated Ships	23
Minesweepers – Coastal	121	Fleet Replenishment Ships	4
Minesweepers – Inshore	100	Tankers	24
LSTs	12	Harbour Tankers	18
LCTs	60	Salvage Vessels	19
LCUs	81	Rescue Ships	15
Depot and Repair Ships	61	Training Ships	27
Intelligence Collectors (AGI)	54	Lifting Ships	15
		Icebreakers (Nuclear)	4
Survey Ships	97	Icebreakers	38
Research Ships	32	Cable Ships	6
Fishery Research Ships	192	Large Tugs	120

Building Programme

The following is an abstract of the programme used in estimating force levels.

Aircraft Carriers
2 Kuril class building as start of continuing programme.

Submarines
Continuing programme for Delta II, Delta, Charlie, Victor, Uniform and Tango classes

Cruisers
Continuing programme for Kara and Kresta II classes

Destroyers
Krivak class continues

Corvettes
Grisha and Nanuchka class continues

Light Forces
New Turya class hydrofoil continues

Minewarfare Forces
New Sonya class (MSC). Natya class continues

Amphibious Forces
New class of LCTs under construction

Air Cushion Vehicles
A large programme of unknown size

Support and Depot Ships
Amur and Ugra classes continuing
New Amga class

AGIs
One extra Moma class

Subsequent types and classes have been revised from new information, not necessarily as new construction.

Deletions and Conversions

Whilst it is not possible to provide an accurate estimate of total deletions and conversions during 1974–75 the following is a guide to the estimates used.

Submarines

Echo 1 converted from SSGN to SSN
Decrease of 10 Whisky class

Destroyers

Kashin class conversions with SSM
1 Krupny class conversion to Kanin class
Kildin class conversions continue

Frigates

Possible conversion of Kola class to auxiliaries

Corvettes

Conversion of some Grisha class to all-gun ships
Deletion of 3 Kronstadt class

Fast Attack Craft

Deletion of 10 Komar class
Deletion of 20 P6, 8 and 10 classes
Deletion of 5 P4 class

Mine Warfare Forces

Deletion of 5 T 301 class

Support Ships

2 Tovda class deleted

Aircraft Carriers

Despite a keen interest in naval aviation, centred largely on flying boats, the Czar's navy made no move to produce an embarked air force. In the immediate post-war years little was seen of an advance in any direction but with the need for national defence as a major priority it was not long before this trend was reversed. Moving through a period when attention was still focussed on flying-boats and sea-planes, of which several hundred were built, the emphasis changed to land-based fighters and bombers. In 1937, when the naval air force numbered some thousand aircraft, an intention to construct aircraft carriers was built into the Third Five Year Plan. The problems of the design of such a ship and the aircraft to fly from her were such that the start of construction was scheduled for 1942. This suggests that the earlier reports of the conversion of an elderly cruiser hull (*Admiral Kornilov*), which was originally laid down at Nikolaev in 1914, remained suspended until 1929 and was then redesigned as a 9,000-ton, 22-aircraft ship named *Stalin*, were premature. Later reports of two 12,000-ton carriers, *Krasnoye-Znamya* and *Voroshilov*, being laid down at Leningrad in 1939–40 were, also, probably premature. These were said to be designed to carry forty aircraft and to have a speed of 30 knots and an armament of twelve 4-inch guns. No trace of these ships was ever seen by outside observers and it must be assumed that they got no further than did the Soviet request to Germany for the plans of the *Graf Zeppelin* or the projected class of two seaplane carriers to be built in the late 1930s.

The first aircraft carrier to sail under Soviet control was the salved ex-German *Graf Zeppelin*, but her voyage was short. The studies for the 1942 carriers were certainly ignored in 1945 when, grossly overloaded with plundered railway trains and other heavy equipment, she foundered under tow in a Baltic storm. From then on the attitude of the Soviet navy to the aircraft carriers appears somewhat ambivalent. Some writings stress the necessity for such a type of ship – others pour scorn on these monsters. But in 1967 came the first Soviet ship ever built with a flight deck, *Moskva*. At 18,000 tons and capable of carrying at least eighteen large helicopters, she was clearly designed for A/S purposes. Allowing for a lead-time of eight to nine years the decision to build this class must have been reached at about the same time as the first of the USN Polaris submarines were laid down. One cannot believe that the original plan was for only the two which eventually appeared, but it seems not unlikely that at least two years before *Moskva* was completed the decision was taken to build the "Kuril" class. This 35,000-ton design with a probable capacity for some fifty aircraft has an angled through-deck with the island offset to starboard as opposed to the centre-line upperworks of the *Moskva*. Although the flight-deck does not extend forward of the bridge this is clearly an aircraft carrier capable of handling VTOL aircraft and helicopters. The Soviet type-name of "anti-submarine cruiser" is presumably designed to circumvent the fact that the Montreux Convention prohibits the passage of aircraft carriers through the Bosphorus, Marmara and Dardanelles. Some cruiser!

AIRCRAFT CARRIERS

Kiev,
Minsk

1 + 1 "Kuril" Class

Displacement, tons	35,000–40,000
Length, feet (*metres*)	925 (*282*) oa; 880 (*268*) wl; 100 (*30·5*) (hull)
Beam, feet (*metres*)	200 (*61*) (overall, including flight deck and sponsons)
Aircraft (estimated)	25 fixed wing (? *Freehand* type) 25 *Hormone*-A or modified *Hind*-A helicopters
Missile launchers	2 twin SAN-3 for *Goblet* missiles; 1 ASW twin launcher; possibly 3-4 SAN-4 launchers
Guns	28 57-mm (see note)
A/S weapons	2 12-barrelled MBU launchers forward
Speed, knots	At least 30

The *Kiev*, and her sister building at the same yard at Nikolayev mark an impressive and logical advance by the Soviet Navy. The arrival of these ships has been heralded by Admiral Gorshkov's support for embarked tactical air as a necessity for navies employed in extending political influence far abroad, and by a softening of previous Soviet criticisms of this class of ship.

    Kiev appears to be a carrier designed for VTOL aircraft and helicopter operations. There is at present no sign of steam catapults, arrester gear, mirror-landing-sights, and all the expensive gear required for fixed-wing operations. Nor is there yet any evidence of the existence of a fixed-wing aircraft suitable for carrier operations. On the other hand, the *Freehand* VTOL aircraft or its derivative, the *Hormone*-A helicopter or a modification of the Army's *Hind*-A helicopter could all be embarked. Two examples of the VTOL aircraft, designed by Yakovlev, appeared at the 1967 Domodedovo air show, were clearly subsonic and mounted 16-round rocket packs under each wing in one aircraft. They were powered by twin turbojet engines, had a wide fuselage to

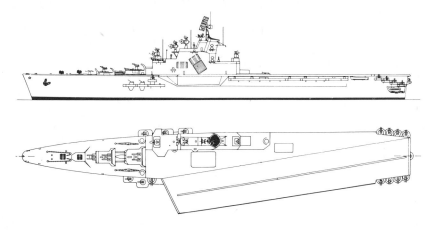

accommodate these and short delta wings of about 27 ft wing-span. The overall length of the aircraft was about 58 ft. Since 1967 further trials of what is apparently an improved version of *Freehand* have continued at Ramenskoye airfield near Moscow, culminating in sea-trials from a specially fitted pad on the flight deck of *Moskva*. These were primarily in the Black Sea – her subsequent deployment to the Mediterranean may have indicated "stage two" in these trials. The provision of a 550–600-ft angled flight deck in the *Kiev* would allow the VTOL aircraft an increase of up to 25% in their take-off weight.

A rough estimate of her hangar capacity suggests that *Kiev* could carry 25 of each type simultaneously. Her forward lift appears to be adequate to accommodate a *Freehand* type but until more detailed evidence is available this, with many other deductions, must remain conjectural. Her armament is of interest, her missiles being, if present estimates are correct, similar to those in *Moskva* with the addition of SAN-4 whilst she may carry a heavy armament of medium-calibre guns. The missile systems, SAN-3, using *Goblet* missiles with a slant range of some 20 miles, are possibly to balance the lack of embarked high-performance fighters and are of longer range than the BPDMSs with Sea Sparrow which are fitted in the latest US carriers. The heavy gun armament is a complete break with the latter's armament – neither *Nimitz* nor *Enterprise* carry any guns. But provision of an increasingly heavy conventional gun-armament can be seen throughout the Soviet surface fleet and this class could be a prime example of this trend.

If *Kiev* turns out to have similar A/S weapons to *Moskva* (twin A/S rocket launchers forward and a possible A/S weapon launcher) another radical change in carrier practice will have been seen. The A/S rocket launchers would presuppose a sonar fit of a hull-mounted set and/or VDS, showing the Soviets have taken the submarine threat seriously. Success with such a system depends very largely on the speed and handling of that ship and the efficiency of the A/S helicopters which, presumably, would work with the weapon launcher.

With world-wide Soviet deployments a pair of ships is clearly insufficient, allowing for maintenance and any refitting required. A minimum of six would be not unlikely.

They will be a powerful addition to the political impact of the Soviet fleet in peacetime. With ships capable of operating VTOL strike aircraft and troop-lift helicopters their credibility in the intervention role would be increased, and their fleet would be that much more prepared for hostilities. Such ships' roles could be changed merely by alterations in the number and type of aircraft embarked. They are clearly not as enormously expensive as the US nuclear-powered carriers but will greatly enhance the manifest capability of the Soviet fleet to operate effectively world-wide in both peace and war.

Gunnery. There is some doubt about the main battery. It may turn out to be a lesser number of 76-mm backed by some 57-mm.

Radar. *Top Sail* and *Headlight*.

Sonar. Possibly hull-mounted and VDS.

Soviet Type Name. *Protivo Lodochny Kreyser* meaning Anti-submarine Cruiser. This is an interesting designation for a ship of this size, suggesting a bias towards A/S in her future employment but more probably aimed at circumventing the restrictions on aircraft carriers in the Montreux Convention, regulating the use of the Turkish Straits.

Leningrad, Moskva

HELICOPTER CRUISERS

2 "Moskva" Class

Displacement, tons	15,000 standard; 17,000 full load
Length, feet (*metres*)	624·8 (*190·5*); 644·8 (*196·6*) oa
Flight deck, feet (*m*)	295·3 (*90·0*) aft of superstructure
Width, feet (*metres*)	115·0 (*35·0*)
Beam, feet (*metres*)	75·9 (*2·0*)
Draught, feet (*metres*)	24·9 (*7·6*)
Aircraft	18 *Hormone*-A ASW helicopters
Missile launchers	2 surface-to-air SAN-3 systems of twin launchers (180 reloads) and 1 twin launcher for anti-submarine missiles
Guns	4 57-mm (2 twin mountings)
A/S weapons	2 12-tube MBUs on forecastle
Torpedo tubes	2 quintuple 21-inch

Main engines	Geared turbines; 2 shafts; 100,000 shp
Boilers	4 watertube
Speed, knots	30 max
Complement	800

Both built at Nikolayev, *Moskva* probably being laid down in 1962–63 as she carried out sea-trials in mid-1967. This class represented a radical change of thought in the Soviet fleet. The design must have been in hand while the "November" class submarines were building and with her heavy A/S armament and efficient sensors (helicopters and VDS) suggests an awareness of the problem of dealing with nuclear submarines. Alongside what is apparently a primary A/S role these ships have a capability for A/A warning and self-defence as well as a command function. With a full fit of radar and ECM equipment they clearly represent good value for money. Both ships handle well in heavy weather and are capable of helicopter-operations under adverse conditions.

Modification. In early 1973 *Moskva* was seen with a landing pad on the after end of the flight-deck, probably for flight tests of VTOL aircraft.

Radar. Search: *Top Sail* 3-D and *Head Net*-C 3-D. Fire control: *Head Light* (2) and *Muff Cob*. Miscellaneous: Electronic warfare equipment.

Sonar. VDS and hull-mounted set. In addition all helicopters have dunking-sonar.

Soviet Type Name. *Protivo Lodochny Kreyser* meaning Anti-submarine Cruiser.

"Moskva" class helicopter cruiser *Leningrad*

Submarines

When war was declared in 1914 Russia had at least thirty submarines in commission and before many months had passed at least another twenty-five were on order. It was the remnant of this large fleet which was to be the founder of the Soviet submarine force of today. By 1922 their numbers had been reduced to seventeen and by 1924 only nine were listed, all refitted in the shipyards which were by then recovering from the damage inflicted during the war. Within two years sufficient advance had been made in these yards for the Defence Council to take the first step towards implementing the decision of the 10th Party Congress of March 1921 to "take measures toward the revival and strengthening of the Red Navy". In 1926 it approved a programme which contained twelve submarines and this was further legitimised by the emphasis placed on these craft in the First Five Year Plan (1928–33). The "Deka-brist" class was started at the Ordzhonikidze Yard, Leningrad, in March 1927, a 1,300-ton design which carried eight torpedo tubes and a crew of forty-four. Although this class was a follow-on of the war-time designs it was interesting in having a deep bridge structure offering more protection than any other design at that time, probably a reflection of these boats' coastal-protection task in the icy waters of the Baltic and, in some cases, the North.

From this time the submarine programme progressed at an increasing tempo. Certain design changes resulted from an interchange with Germany and the salving of the British L55 which had been sunk off Kronstadt in 1919. By 1940 there were 160 submarines listed, the largest submarine force in the world.

When Hitler invaded the USSR in June 1941 the total had risen to 180 and this was to be steadily increased during the next four years from the building yards at Molotovsk (near Archangel), Gorky (300 miles East of Moscow on the Volga) and Komsomolsk (300 miles up the Amur River in the Far East). The main surface-ship building areas suffered most from the German advance and it was these three widely dispersed submarine yards which were the scene of the majority of Soviet naval construction between 1941 and 1945. Thus, in the post-war years of rehabilitation, they were in a position to provide a large proportion of the building work needed to implement Stalin's direction of July 1945 to provide a "still stronger and more powerful navy".

Of the boats comprising the 1941 fleet only the "Pravda" class at 1,800 tons had exceeded the average medium range of 1,400 tons. This huge number of submarines had made little impact during the war. Deprived of their experienced officers by Stalin's purges in the late 1930s, operating with inadequate sensors and manned by crews whose technical capability was at an astonishingly low level even in 1945 their patrols were, on the whole, incompetently executed and the results minimal. Yet, at a time when morale was low and efficiency far below that acceptable in any Western navy, the submarine fleet continued its expansion programme. Submarines of the "K", "Shckuka", "S" and "Malutka" classes came off the slips in considerable numbers while the designers worked on new plans derived from the captured German Type XXI submarine, the Walther-turbine boats seized in German ports and the knowledge of the numerous German scientists herded back to the USSR.

From all these studies stemmed the first major post-war submarine design, the "Whisky" class. Of 1,350 tons these were smaller boats than the Type XXIs, mounted six tubes and were capable of 15 knots dived. At the time of the first "Whisky's" commissioning in 1951 she was probably the most advanced design then in the water with the exception of the few remaining Type XXIs and the first of the six US "Tang" class, much larger at 2,700 tons. Between 1951 and 1957 no less than 240 of this class were built, eventually appearing in five different forms – I and IV had a gun forward of the conning-tower, II had guns at both ends, III and V had no guns, whilst a later conversion, VA, had a diver's hatch fitted forward of the conning tower.

At almost the same time came the "Zulu" class, a larger edition of the "Whisky". They appeared in four different versions with a fifth, "Zulu V" of seven boats, being the first Soviet ballistic-missile armed class. With the first conversion appearing in 1956 they carried two SSN-4 tubes for *Sark* missiles in the rear of a much enlarged fin whilst the remainder of the structure remained unaltered.

The construction of these two classes was to illustrate a unique element in Soviet planning – with a design approved, mass-production followed. This could always be halted, variations incorporated or conversions put in hand but it resulted in no delay whilst prototypes were evaluated during extensive sea-trials. It is not clear whether this is still the practice but until the last year or so it has been a major factor in the astonishing build-up of the strength of the Soviet submarine force.

At this point in the early 1950s three separate but interlinked lines of development became apparent – those of the attack submarine, the cruise-missile submarine and the ballistic-missile submarine. To avoid confusion these three will be considered separately.

We have seen that the "Whisky" and "Zulu" classes were a radical departure from previous Soviet designs, and stemmed from lessons learned from a study of the recent war. The urgent need for high speed in submarine operations resulted in the "Quebec" class of 740 tons which was powered with two electric motors and, on a third shaft, a Walther-turbine running on High Test Peroxide (HTP). Speeds around 18–19 knots were achieved but apparently similar problems to those met when the Royal Navy tried this form of propulsion caused the replacement of the turbine by a third electric motor. Twenty-two of this class were built, the majority being relegated to a training role and, subsequently, to reserve. In 1958 two more classes appeared, the first of eighteen "Romeo" class and the first of sixty-four "Foxtrot" class. The former, of 1,600 tons, was a development of the "Whisky" and the latter, of 2,300 tons, an advance on the "Zulu". Of these classes a considerable number have been transferred to other navies – fifty-five "Whiskys", six "Romeos" and eight "Foxtrots". The last of these is, probably, with the British "Oberon" class, the most successful diesel-propelled patrol submarine ever produced.

But 1958 was of great importance for another reason – the appearance of the first of the nuclear-driven fleet submarines of the "November" class. In that year, again apparently without a prototype, the lead-boat of a class of fourteen was completed at Severodvinsk. Of the same tonnage as USS *Nautilus* (4,000 tons) these boats were noisy and lacking in design finesse but they were fast at 25 knots and represented a major capability hitherto denied to the Soviet Navy. They were capable of engaging carrier task forces with a far greater chance of success than ever before.

The construction of the "Novembers" continued until 1963 and there was then a break in the building of Fleet submarines until 1967 when the first of the "Victors" appeared. Although shorter (285 ft) by 75 ft than the "Novembers" they were of approximately the same tonnage (4,200 against 4,000 tons) but had a far better hull design and a new nuclear power plant giving a dived speed in excess of 30 knots. Fourteen of these have so far been commissioned and appear to be still the nucleus of the attack submarine force, although the single "Alpha" completed in 1970 and the new "Victor II" class of 1974 may be indicators of further advances. Also of interest is the continuing construction of diesel-propelled submarines, albeit in small numbers. Six of the "Bravo" class have been completed since 1968, boats which may well have a target role. But not so the "Tango", the only observed unit of which appeared at the Sevastopol review in July 1973. She shows all the signs of being a new variety of the pure patrol submarine – perhaps an insurance against steeply rising costs in the nuclear field?

The gap in the fleet submarine programme is possibly accounted for by the emphasis on cruise-missile armed boats during this period. This showed a steady advance from the five "Whisky Twin Cylinder" modifications of 1958–60, a rough-and-ready means of getting two SSN-3

Shaddock missiles to sea in a submarine. With an optimum range probably around 100 miles and requiring mid-course guidance, four of these missiles were mounted in the seven "Whisky Long Bin" conversions of 1960–63, six in the five "Echo I" nuclear-propelled boats of 1960–62, four in the sixteen "Juliet" diesel-propelled boats of 1962–67, and eight in the twenty-seven nuclear boats of the 1963–67 "Echo II" class. Thus by the end of 1967 sixty submarines carrying long-range missiles were available to combat any encroaching carrier task-forces. But two factors must be considered here: in order to fire, these submarines had to surface; furthermore, the main weight of seaborne nuclear retaliation had now been placed on the ballistic-missile armed submarines of which the USN possessed forty-one and the French and British were building their own quota. A new problem had been set the Soviet Navy at a time when the "Victor" class became available for anti-submarine operations. The solution of the difficulties imposed by the requirement to launch missiles on the surface appeared in 1968 with the first of the 5,100 ton "Charlie" class. These were of the same generation of hull and reactor design as the "Victors" and with a speed of over 30 knots and eight tubes for the new short-range dived-launch SSN-7 missiles as well as eight torpedo tubes they rounded off the ingredients of an extremely complex problem for the commander of any surface force to which they were opposed. With long-range missiles capable of launch beyond the fleet's A/S environment, short-range missiles with a range of some twenty-five miles from the "Charlies" and the later "Papa" class and torpedo-firing boats with an extremely high underwater performance, an admiral would be hard-put to dispose his forces to the best advantage.

The last group to be considered represents modern operations completely alien to traditional submarine work – the nuclear-deterrent patrol. The Russians were early in this field, having launched their first submarine-oriented ballistic missile in 1955, two years before the first American SSBN, *George Washington*, was laid down. In 1956 the first submarine in history with a capability of launching any form of ballistic missile was at sea – the "Zulu V" conversion already referred to. This class had twin tubes in the fin which were launchers for the 300-mile range SSN-4 *Sark* missiles. In 1958 came the first of the twenty-two "Golf" class with three *Sark* tubes, also in the fin. They were followed closely by the first of the fifteen nuclear-propelled "Hotel" class with the same weapon load and pre-dating the first US SSBN by over a year. The range of the SSN-4 system was insufficient for sustained operational use and between 1963–67 nine of the "Hotels" were re-armed with the SSN-5 *Serb* system with a 700-mile range. On completion of this programme, half of the "Golfs" were similarly retro-fitted. Both were redesignated "Hotel II" or "Golf II". The reason for only a proportion of these two classes being modernised became evident in late 1967 when the first of thirty-four "Yankee" class SSBNs was commissioned. Of 9,000 tons and 426 feet length, compared to the US "Ethan Allen" class of 7,900 tons and 410 feet, they carried sixteen missile tubes for the SSN-6 *Sawfly* system with a range of 1,300 miles, comparable to the US Polaris A2 missile. But, whilst the range of Polaris was extended by the USN to 2,500 miles with the A3 missile and Poseidon introduced with a similar range, no similar action was noted in the USSR. The reason became clear in 1972. After trials in a converted "Hotel III" class the SSN-8 missile, with a 4,200-mile range, was put to sea in the first of the new "Delta" class. The Soviet Navy now had the capability of striking the USA without the need for its submarines moving beyond the Iceland-Faroes gap – at least six years before it was possible for the USA to deploy its Trident-I missile at sea. This will have a range approaching that of SSN-8 (3,000–4,000 miles) and will be fitted with a MIRV warhead, a development already foreshadowed in the USSR by the Soviet's trials of MRV heads on SSN-6. In 1973 the "Delta II" arrived, probably with at least sixteen tubes. Under the terms of the present Strategic Arms Limitation agreement the Soviets are allowed a maximum of sixty-two modern SSBNs with a total of 950 missiles and the USA 44 SSBNs with 710 missiles.

In sum, therefore, we are presented with the largest peace-time submarine force the world has ever known. On the credit side it has a number of major successes to look back upon – the first mass-produced post-war class of advanced patrol submarines, the first large force of cruise-missile submarines, the first class of Fleet submarines capable of more than 30 knots, the first class of SSBNs carrying missiles with a range greater than 4,000 miles. On the debit side this service, now numbering some 380 submarines, has not yet solved the problem of quiet running for nuclear boats, has not mastered the art of detecting quiet submarines on patrol and, despite the precedence given to submarine-manning, is in a difficult position when it comes to providing the necessary highly-trained ships' companies. Maybe this last is reflected in the fact that a considerable proportion of the Fleet submarines and SSBNs in the Soviet Navy are commanded by senior captains. They have had innumerable problems in the past. Many have been overcome but, in considering their present numerical superiority, it must be remembered that many remain to be solved.

BALLISTIC MISSILE CLASSES

1 + 1 "Delta II" Class
(Ballistic Missile Submarines SSBNs)

This 16,000-ton submarine was first reported in November 1973. With an armament of 16 SSN-18 missile tubes she is by far the largest submarine ever built.

14 + 10 "Delta" Class
(Ballistic Missile Submarines SSBNs)

Displacement, tons	9,000 surfaced; 10,000 dived
Length, feet (*metres*)	450 (*137·2*)
Beam, feet (*metres*)	34·8 (*10·6*)
Draught, feet (*metres*)	32·8 (*10·0*)
Missile launchers	12 SSN-8 tubes
Torpedo tubes	8 21-in
Main machinery	Nuclear reactors; Steam turbines; 2 screws; 24,000 shp
Speed, knots	25
Complement	About 120

This new class of SSBNs was announced at the end of 1972. The missile armament is 12 SSN-8s with a range of 4,200 nautical miles at present believed to carry single heads, rather than MRVs. As the SSN-6 has already been tested with MRV warheads, however, it is not unlikely that these missiles will, in due course, be similarly armed. The longer range SSN-8 missiles are of greater length than the SSN-6s and, as this length can not be accommodated below the keel, they stand several feet proud of the after-casing. At the same time their presumed greater diameter and the need to compensate for the additional top-weight would seem to be the reasons for the reduction to 12 missiles in this class. The total "Delta" class building programme depends on the final outcome of the various Strategic Arms Limitation Talks (SALT). As this is unclear and dependent on so many external influences it is unwise to forecast any figure. A building rate of 10–12 SSBNs per year is well within Soviet capabilities.

34 "Yankee" Class
(Ballistic Missile Submarines SSBNs)

Displacement, tons	8,000 surfaced, 9,000 dived
Length, feet (*metres*)	426·5 (*130·0*)
Beam, feet (*metres*)	34·8 (*10·6*)
Draught, feet (*metres*)	32·8 (*10·0*)
Missile launchers	16 SSN-6 tubes

Torpedo tubes	8 21-in
Main machinery	Nuclear reactors; steam turbines; 24,000 shp
Speed, knots	25
Complement	About 120

The first units of this class were reported in 1968. At about the time that the USS *George Washington* was laid down (1 November 1957) as the world's first SSBN it is likely that the Soviet Navy embarked on its own major SSBN programme. With experience gained from the diesel-propelled "Golf" class and the nuclear-propelled "Hotel" class, both originally carrying 3 SSN-4 (300-mile) missiles in the fin, the "Yankee" design was completed mounting 16 SSN-6 missiles in the hull in two banks of 8. The first of the class was delivered late-1967 and the programme then accelerated from four boats in 1968 to eight in 1971. The original deployment of this class was to the eastern seaboard of the US giving a coverage at least as far as the Mississippi. Increase in numbers allowed a Pacific patrol to be established off California extending coverage at least as far as the Rockies. To provide greater coverage and more flexible operations a longer range missile system was needed and this is now at sea in the "Delta" class.

Missiles. The MOD 1 SSN-6 carries a single head to a range of 1,300 miles. MOD 2 (operational 1974) has a range of 1,600 miles whilst MOD 3 has the same range but carries a MRV head.

1 "Hotel III" Class
8 "Hotel II" Class
(Ballistic Missile Submarines SSBNs)

Displacement, tons	4,400 surfaced; 5,150 dived
Length, feet (*metres*)	377·2 (*115·2*)
Beam, feet (*metres*)	28·2 (*8·6*)
Draught, feet (*metres*)	25 (*7·6*)
Missile launchers	3 SSN-5 tubes
Torpedo tubes	6 21-in (bow); 4 16-in (aft) (anti-submarine)
Main machinery	Nuclear reactor; steam turbine; 22,500 shp
Speed, knots	20 (dived)
Complement	90

Long-range submarines with three vertical ballistic-missile tubes in the large fin for surface launch. All this class were completed between 1958 and 1962. Originally fitted with SSN-4 system with *Sark* missiles (300 miles). Between 1963 and 1967 this system was replaced by the SSN-5 system with *Serb*

"Hotel II" class

missiles capable of 700-mile range. Since then these boats have been deployed off both coasts of the USA and Canada. As the limitations of SALT are felt the "Hotel IIs" will probably be phased out to allow the maximum number of "Delta" class to be built.

The "Hotel III" was a single unit converted for the test firings of the SSN-8. The earlier boats of this class, which was of a similar hull and reactor design to the "Echo" class, will, by the late 1970s, be reaching their twentieth year in service.

22 "Golf I and II" Class
(Ballistic Missile Submarines SSB)

Displacement, tons	2,350 surfaced; 2,800 dived
Length, feet (*metres*)	320·0 (*97·5*)
Beam, feet (*metres*)	25·1 (*7·6*)
Draught, feet (*metres*)	22·0 (*6·7*)
Missile launchers	3 SSN-4 tubes (G 1), 3 SSN-5 tubes (G II)
Torpedo tubes	10 21-in (6 bow, 4 stern)
Main machinery	3 diesels; 3 shafts; 6,000 hp; Electric motors; 6,000 hp
Speed, knots	17·6 surfaced; 17 dived
Range, miles	22,700 surfaced, cruising
Complement	86 (12 officers, 74 men)

This type has a very large fin fitted with three vertically-mounted tubes and hatches for surface launch of ballistic missiles. Built at Komsomolsk and Severodvinsk. Building started in 1958 and finished in 1961-62. After the missile conversion of the "Hotel" class was completed in 1967 about half this

"Golf I" class

class was converted to carry the SSN-5 system with 700-mile range *Serb* missiles in place of the shorter-range (300-mile) *Sarks*. One of this class has been built by China, although apparently lacking missiles.

1 "Zulu V" Class
(Ex-Ballistic Missile Submarine SSB)

"Zulu V" class

Displacement, tons	2,100 surfaced; 2,600 dived
Length, feet (*metres*)	259·3 (*90·0*)
Beam, feet (*metres*)	24·1 (*7·3*)
Draught, feet (*metres*)	19·0 (*5·8*)
Missile launchers	2 SSN-4 tubes
Torpedo tubes	10 21–in
Main machinery	3 diesels; 3 shafts; 10,000 bhp; 3 electric motors; 3,500 hp
Range, miles	13,000 surfaced, cruising
Speed, knots	18 surfaced; 15 dived
Complement	85

These were basically of "Z" class design but converted in 1956–57 to ballistic-missile submarines with larger fins and two vertical tubes for launching *Sark* (300-mile) missiles on the surface. These were the first Soviet ballistic-missile submarines. Of the six converted only one remains on the list. Three others have been converted for research duties as *Lira*, *Orion* and *Vega* whilst two more may have been converted back to patrol submarines.

CRUISE MISSILE CLASSES

1 "Papa" Class
(Cruise Missile Submarines SSGN)

A new class of nuclear submarine, generally similar to the earlier "Charlie" class. First reported in 1972.

12 "Charlie" Class
(Cruise Missile Submarine SSGN)

Displacement, tons	4,000 surfaced; 5,100 dived
Length, feet (*metres*)	304·8 (*94*)
Beam, feet (*metres*)	32·8 (*10·0*)
Draught, ft (*m*)	24·6 (*7·5*)
Missile launchers	8 SSN-7 tubes
Torpedo tubes	8 21-in
Main machinery	Nuclear reactor; steam turbines; 24,000 shp
Speed, knots	30 approx, dived; 20 surfaced
Complement	100

"Charlie" class

A class of cruise-missile submarine building at Gorky at a rate of about three per year. The first of class was delivered in 1968, representing a very significant advance in the cruise-missile submarine field. With a speed of at least 30 knots and mounting eight missile tubes for the SSN-7 system (30-mile range) which has a dived launch capability, this is a great advance on the "Echo" class. Having an improved hull and reactor design these boats must be assumed to have an organic control for their missile system and therefore pose a notable threat to any surface force. Their deployment to the Mediterranean, the area of the US 6th Fleet, suggests their probable employment. The only strange thing about them is their comparatively low building rate.

27 "Echo II" Class
(Cruise Missile Submarines SSGN)

Displacement, tons	4,800 surfaced; 5,600 dived
Length, feet (*metres*)	390·7 (*119*)
Beam, feet (*metres*)	28·4 (*8·6*)
Draught, feet (*metres*)	25·9 (*7·9*)
Missile launchers	8 SSN-3 tubes

Torpedo tubes	6 21-in (bow); 4 16-in (aft)
Main machinery	Nuclear reactor; steam turbine; 22,500 shp
Speed, knots	20
Complement	100

The "Echo II" was the natural development of the "Echo I". With a slightly lengthened hull, a fourth pair of launchers was installed and between 1963 and 1967 twenty-seven of this class were built. They are now deployed evenly between the Pacific and Northern fleets and still provide a useful group of boats for operations such as those of the mixed task force which was in the South China Sea in June 1972. As well as surface ships this included three "Echo IIs" and an "Echo I".

"Echo II" class

16 "Juliet" Class
(Cruise Missile Submarines SSG)

Displacement, tons	3,200 surfaced; 3,600 dived
Length, feet (*metres*)	285·4 (*87*)
Beam, feet (*metres*)	31·4 (*9·5*)
Draught, feet (*metres*)	20·0 (*6·1*)
Missile launchers	4 SSN-3 tubes; 2 before and 2 abaft the fin
Torpedo tubes	6 21-in (bow); 2 or 4 16-in (aft)
Main machinery	Diesels; 6,000 bhp. Electric motors; 6,000 hp
Speed, knots	16 surfaced; 16 dived
Range, miles	15,000 surfaced, cruising

Completed between 1962 and 1967. An unmistakable class with a high casing to house the four SSN-3 launchers, one pair either end of the fin which appears to be comparatively low. This class was the logical continuation of the "Whisky" class conversions but was overtaken by the "Echo" class SSGNs. A number of this class has in the past been deployed to the Mediterranean.

"Juliet" class

7 "Whisky Long-Bin" Class
(Cruise Missile Submarines SSG)

Displacement, tons	1,200 surfaced; 1,800 dived
Length, feet (*metres*)	275·6 (*84*)
Beam, feet (*metres*)	19·8 (*6·0*)
Draught, feet (*metres*)	15·7 (*4·8*)
Missile launchers	4 SSN-3 tubes
Torpedo tubes	6 21-in (4 bow, 2 stern)
Main machinery	Diesels; 4,000 bhp. Electric motors; 2,500 hp
Speed, knots	17 surfaced; 15 dived
Range, miles	13,000 surfaced, cruising

"Whisky Twin
Cylinder" class

A more efficient modification of the "Whisky" class than the Twin-Cylinder with four SSN-3 launchers built into a remodelled fin on a hull lengthened by 26 feet. Converted between 1960–63. No organic guidance and therefore reliance must be made on aircraft or surface-ship cooperation. Must be a very noisy boat when dived.

5 "Whisky Twin Cylinder" Class
(Cruise Missile Submarines SSG)

Displacement, tons	1,100 surfaced; 1,600 dived
Length, feet (*metres*)	247 (*75·3*)
Beam, feet (*metres*)	19·0 (*5·8*)
Draught, feet (*metres*)	15·1 (*4·6*)
Missile launchers	2 SSN-3 tubes
Torpedo tubes	6 21-in (4 bow, 2 stern)
Main machinery	Diesels; 4,000 bhp; Electric motors; 2,500 hp
Speed, knots	17 surface; 15 submerged
Range, miles	13,000 surfaced, cruising

A 1958–60 modification of the conventional "Whisky" class designed to test out the SSN-3 system at sea. The modification consisted of fitting a pair of launchers abaft the fin. Probably never truly operational being a thoroughly messy conversion which must make an excessive noise when proceeding at any speed above dead slow when dived.

FLEET SUBMARINE CLASSES

1 "Alpha" Class
(Fleet Submarine SSN)

Displacement, tons	3,500 surfaced; 4,500 dived

One unit of this class was completed in 1970. Her form of propulsion is by no means certain nor is her purpose. It is, however, believed that this is a "one-off" nuclear boat.

1 "Victor II" Class
(Fleet Submarine SSN)

Displacement, tons	4,700 tons surfaced; 6,000 dived
Length, feet (*metres*)	331·3 (*101*)

One unit of a new class of nuclear-propelled submarine has been reported. This is believed to be an enlarged edition of the "Victor" class.

16 "Victor" Class
(Fleet Submarines SSN)

Displacement, tons	4,200 surfaced; 5,100 dived
Length, feet (*metres*)	285·4 (*87·0*)
Beam, feet (*metres*)	32·8 (*10·0*)
Draught, feet (*metres*)	26·2 (*8·0*)
Torpedo tubes	8 21-in
Main machinery	Nuclear reactor; steam turbines; 24,000 shp
Speed, knots	26 surfaced; 30+ dived

Designed purely as a torpedo-carrying submarine its much increased speed makes it a menace to all but the fastest ships. The first of class entered service in 1967–68 with a subsequent building rate of about two per year. The majority is deployed with the Northern Fleet, although two have joined the Pacific Fleet.

"Victor" class

"November" class

13 "November" Class
(Fleet Submarines SSN)

Displacement, tons	4,200 surfaced; 4,800 dived
Length, feet (*metres*)	360·9 (*110·0*)
Beam, feet (*metres*)	32·1 (*9·8*)
Draught, feet (*metres*)	24·3 (*7·4*)
Torpedo tubes	6 21-in (bow)
Main machinery	Nuclear reactor; steam turbines; 22,500 shp
Speed, knots	20 surfaced; 25 dived
Complement	88

The first class of Soviet Fleet submarines which entered service between 1958 and 1963. The hull form with the great number of free-flood holes in the casing suggests a noisy boat and it is surprising that greater efforts have not been made to supersede this class with the "Victors". In 1970 one of this class sank south-west of the United Kingdom.

Class Name. Reported as *Leninsky Komsomol.*

Diving Depth. Reported as 1,650 feet (*500 metres*).

1 "Echo I" Class
(Fleet Submarine SSN)

Displacement, tons	4,600 surfaced; 5,000 dived
Length, feet (*metres*)	380·9 (*116·0*)
Beam, feet (*metres*)	28·4 (*8·6*)
Draught, feet (*metres*)	25·9 (*7·9*)
Torpedo tubes	6 21-in (bow); 4 16-in (aft)
Main machinery	Nuclear reactor; steam turbine; 22,500 shp
Speed, knots	20
Complement	92 (12 officers; 80 men)

This class was completed in 1960–62. Originally mounted six SSN-3 launchers raised from the after casing. The hull of this class is very similar to the "Hotel" "November" type and it is probably powered by similar nuclear plant. This class was started at about the same time as the "Juliet" diesel-driven SSGs, and may have been intended as a nuclear prototype using the same SSN-3 system. Only five "Echo Is" were built, probably an adequate test for a new weapon system, being followed immediately by the "Echo IIs". In 1973–74 the last of the "Echo I" class was converted into a fleet submarine with the removal of the missile system.

"Echo I" class
(as SSN)

PATROL SUBMARINE CLASSES

3 "Tango" Class
(Patrol Submarine SS)

Displacement, tons	1,900 surfaced; 2,500 dived
Length, feet (*metres*)	300·0 (*92·0*)
Beam, feet (*metres*)	30·0 (*9·1*)
Draught, feet (*metres*)	16·0 (*4·9*)
Complement	60

This class was first seen at the Sevastopol review in July 1973. Notable features are the rise in the forecasing and a new shape for the snort exhaust. This class, following five years after the "Bravo", shows a continuing commitment to diesel-propelled boats which is of interest in view of the comparatively slow Fleet submarine building programme. If the USSR wishes to maintain a preponderance in numbers as the more elderly patrol submarines are paid off this may be the class chosen for new construction. It would also provide a modern replacement for client nations' navies. Now in series production.

4 "Bravo" Class
(Patrol Submarines SS)

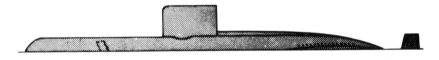

Displacement, tons	2,500 surfaced; 2,800 dived
Length, feet (*metres*)	229·6 (*70·0*)
Beam, feet (*metres*)	24·8 (*7·5*)
Draught, feet (*metres*)	14·8 (*4·5*)
Torpedo tubes	6 21-in (?)
Main machinery	Diesel-Electric
Speed, knots	16 dived

The drawing is merely an indication of the general form which this class may be expected to have. The beam-to-length ratio is larger than normal in a diesel submarine which would account in part for the large displacement for a comparatively short hull.

First completed in 1968 – built at Northern and Baltic yards. One attached to each of the main fleets, reinforcing the view that these are "padded targets" for torpedo and A/S firings.

56 "Foxtrot" Class
(Patrol Submarines SS)

Displacement, tons	2,000 surfaced; 2,300 dived
Length, feet (*metres*)	301·7 (*92*)
Beam, feet (*metres*)	24·1 (*7·3*)
Draught, feet (*metres*)	19·0 (*5·8*)
Torpedo tubes	10 21-in (6 bow, 4 stern); 20 torpedoes carried
Main machinery	Diesels; 3 shafts; 6,000 bhp. 3 electric motors; 6,000 hp
Speed, knots	20 surfaced; 15 dived
Complement	70
Range, miles	20,000 surfaced, cruising

Built between 1958 and 1967 at Sudomekh and Leningrad. A follow-on from the "Zulu" class with similar propulsion to the "Golf" class. A most successful class which has been deployed world-wide, forming the bulk of the Soviet submarine force in the Mediterranean. Four transferred to India in 1968–70 with a further four new construction following in 1973–75.

"Foxtrot" class

12 "Romeo" Class
(Patrol Submarines SS)

Displacement, tons	1,000 surfaced; 1,600 dived
Length, feet (*metres*)	249·3 (*76*)
Beam, feet (*metres*)	24·0 (*7·3*)
Draught, feet (*metres*)	14·5 (*4·4*)
Torpedo tubes	6 21-in bow
Main machinery	Diesels; 4,000 bhp. Electric motors; 4,000 hp; 2 shafts
Speed, knots	17 surfaced; 14 dived
Complement	65

These are an improved "W" class design with modernised conning tower and sonar installation. A total of eighteen was built between 1958 and 1961. This was presumably an interim class while the "November" class of Fleet Submarines was brought into service – an insurance against failure. Six of this class transferred to Egypt in 1966 and the Chinese are building a considerable force of the same class of submarines.

"Romeo" class

19 + 3 "Zulu IV" Class
(Patrol Submarines SS)

Displacement, tons	2,000 surfaced; 2,200 dived
Length, feet (*metres*)	259·3 (*90·0*)
Beam, feet (*metres*)	23·9 (*7·3*)
Draught, feet (*metres*)	19·0 (*5·8*)
Torpedo tubes	10 21–in (6 bow, 4 stern); 24 torpedoes or 40 mines carried
Main machinery	Diesel-electric; 3 shafts, 3 diesels; 10,000 bhp. 3 electric motors; 3,500 hp
Speed, knots	18 surfaced; 15 dived
Range, miles	20,000 surfaced, cruising
Complement	70

The first large post-war patrol submarines built by USSR. Completed from late 1951 to 1955. General appearance is streamlined with a complete row of free-flood holes along the casing. Eighteen were built by Sudomekh Shipyard, Leningrad, in 1952–55 and the other eight at Severodvinsk. The general external similarity to the later German U-boats of WWII suggests that this was not an entirely indigenous design. All now appear to be of the "Zulu IV" type. This class, although the majority are probably still operational, is obsolescent and will soon be disposed of.

The six "Zulu V" conversions, which started in 1956, of this class provided the first Soviet ballistic missile submarines with SSN-4 systems.

100 "Whisky" Class
(Patrol Submarines SS)

Displacement, tons	1,030 surfaced; 1,350 dived
Length, feet (*metres*)	249·3 (*76*)
Beam, feet (*metres*)	22·0 (*6·7*)
Draught, feet (*metres*)	15·0 (*4·6*)
Torpedo tubes	6 21–in (4 bow, 2 stern); 18 torpedoes or 40 mines carried
Main machinery	Diesel-electric; 2 shafts; Diesels; 4,000 bhp. Electric motors; 2,500 hp
Speed, knots	17 surfaced; 15 dived
Range, miles	13,000 at 8 knots (surfaced)
Complement	60

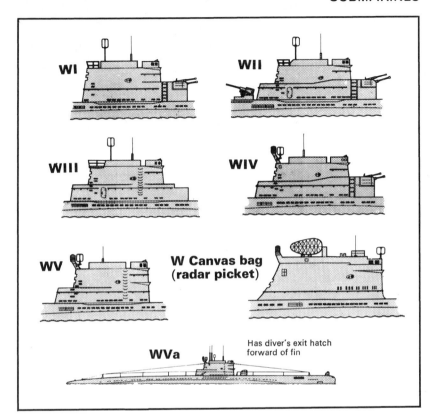

WI

WII

WIII

WIV

WV

W Canvas bag (radar picket)

WVa   Has diver's exit hatch forward of fin

"Whisky V" class

This was the first post-war Soviet design for a medium-range submarine. Like its larger contemporary the "Zulu", this class shows considerable German influence. About 240 of the "Whiskys" were built between 1951 and 1957 at yards throughout the USSR. Built in six types – I and IV had guns forward of the conning tower, II had guns both ends, whilst III and V have no guns. V is the most common variant whilst VA has a diver's exit hatch forward of the conning tower. Now being paid-off at possibly fifteen to twenty per year. Up to 50% are probably now in reserve.

Two of this class, named *Severyanka* and *Slavyanka*, were converted for oceanographic and fishery research.

Foreign Transfers. Has been the most popular export model and is currently in service in Albania (4), Bulgaria (2), China (21), Egypt (6), Indonesia (4), North Korea (4) and Poland (4).

3 "Whisky Canvas Bag" Class
(Radar Picket Submarines SSR)

Displacement, tons	1,100 surfaced; 1,200 dived
Length, feet (*metres*)	240·0 (*73·2*)
Beam, feet (*metres*)	22·0 (*6·7*)
Draught, feet (*metres*)	15·0 (*4·6*)
Torpedo tubes	6 21-in (4 bow, 2 stern)
Main machinery·	Diesels; 4,000 bhp. Electric motors; 2,500 hp
Speed, knots	17 surfaced; 15 dived
Range, miles	13,000 at 8 knots (surfaced)
Complement	65

Basically of same design as the "Whisky" class but with long-range *Boat-Sail* radar aerial mounted on the fin. The coy way in which this was covered prompted the title "Canvas Bag". Converted between 1959–1963.

22 "Quebec" Class
(Patrol Submarines SS)

Short-range, coastal submarines. Built from 1954 to 1957. Thirteen were constructed in 1955 by Sudomekh Shipyard, Leningrad. The earlier boats of this class were fitted with a form of Walther turbine on the third shaft. It is believed to have been unsuccessful and subsequently removed. The majority of this class are now in reserve.

SUBMARINES

Displacement, tons	650 surfaced; 740 dived
Length, feet (*metres*)	185·0 (*56·4*)
Length, feet (*metres*)	18·0 (*5·5*)
Draught, feet (*metres*)	13·2 (*4·0*)
Torpedo tubes	4 21-in bow
Main machinery	1 diesel; 3 shafts; 3,000 bhp. 3 electric motors; 2,500 hp
Speed, knots	18 surfaced; 16 dived
Oil fuel, tons	50
Range, miles	7,000 surfaced, cruising
Complement	42

Cruisers

At no time in the 20th Century has the Russian Fleet been without its cruisers. Eleven were lost in the Russo–Japanese War of 1904–05 – a like number survived. In the traumatic period which followed this crippling defeat little was done to replace these losses and it was more than five years later before any considerable building programme was approved. This dilatoriness was reflected in the shipyards so that in 1914 eighteen cruisers were still under construction (two in Germany). After the war and the Revolution we have already seen that the Soviet Navy was in a state of considerable disarray – two cruisers survived in 1924 and three more of modified war-time design were completed over the next eight years.

In 1935 the lead pair of the 9,000-ton "Kirov" class, the first cruisers designed for the new Soviet Navy, were laid down. Six of these were completed, four before the war began in June 1941 and two at Komsomolosk in 1944; their appearance gave clear indication of the considerable Italian assistance in their planning.

A further six ships of the larger "Frunze" or "Chapaev" class were laid down between 1938–40 but construction was suspended during the war, only five being completed after 1945. These were large ships of 15,000 tons and show a considerable similarity in appearance, armament and propulsion to their successors, the first post-1945 design, the 18,000 ton "Sverdlovs". Twenty-four of these were planned, twenty laid down, seventeen launched and fourteen completed. Their completion dates spanned the time when Khruschev, newly in charge after the power struggle following Stalin's death, had set his face against big ships. By what means the new C-in-C, Admiral Gorshkov, managed to save even fourteen hulls from the imbroglio we do not know but it seems little short of a miracle.

The "Sverdlovs" were the last cruiser design in which the gun retained its position as the main armament. With the first surface-to-surface missiles (SSMs) put to sea in the "Kildin" (1957) and "Krupny" (1959) class destroyers the Soviet Navy built the "Kynda" class cruisers. With eight launcher tubes in a 6,000-ton hull, she was laid down in June 1960 at the Zhdanov yard, Leningrad, being completed two years later. The interest in this class is that they were the first missile-carrying ships which were apparently purpose-built – both the destroyer classes used "Kotlin" class hulls. They have separate guidance systems for each of the SSN-3 launchers but to use them at their optimum range (100 miles–maximum range more than 400 miles) mid-course guidance from another ship, submarine or aircraft was needed. For anti-aircraft defence a twin surface-to-air (SAM) missile launcher was mounted forward with two twin 76-mm guns aft. This somewhat insignificant total suggests that the "Kyndas" were designed to operate under shore-based air cover and were thus severely limited in their range of operations. The reason for their construction was clearly to counter-attack NATO carrier groups which might threaten the USSR with aircraft armed with nuclear weapons. As the operating radius of the largest US carrier-borne aircraft designed for nuclear strike which was available in the mid-1950s (the AJ-1 Savage) was about 1,000 miles these carrier groups were forced to enter the Norwegian Sea or Eastern Mediterranean before launching their aircraft. As both areas were within range of Soviet shore-based aircraft the design of the "Kynda" was probably tactically sound although, operationally, very limiting. The decision to design such a class must have been reached in 1954 at the latest to allow for a Soviet type lead-time before completion of the first ship. It may thus have been one of the earliest main decisions of the Gorshkov era.

It is unlikely that only four (the number eventually completed) was the total originally planned for the "Kyndas". Later evidence suggests that ten to a dozen were programmed. But at hull four the programme was stopped and replaced by the "Kresta I" class. The first of these was laid down at Zhdanov in September 1964, the result of a staff requirement which must have been formulated in 1958 at the latest. Now this class showed the first evidence of a determination on the part of the Naval Staff to produce a class of ship capable of operating in more distant waters. The eight SSN-3 launchers were reduced to two twin mounts forward, the number of SAN-1 launchers was doubled, the calibre of the guns reduced from 76-mm to 57-mm giving a greater number of rounds in the same magazine space, the A/S equipment and weapons were improved and, most important, a helicopter hangar and flight deck were provided aft. The "Kresta I" could, therefore, operate much further from her own bases with some prospect of survival, at least until her missiles were launched, possessing the essential capability for mid-course guidance of these missiles by the use of her own helicopter.

But only four "Kresta Is" were completed. The arrival of the first of the "Kresta II" class in 1969 showed why. Yet another change in tactical thought had taken place and this must have been in about 1962. Just larger than her predecessor at 7,500 tons and with a marginal improvement in range, she retained the helicopter and A/S weapons of her predecessors. But four small-calibre guns of a new design were added and, although the SAM armament was unchanged, the long-range SSN-3 system was replaced by two quadruple launchers for the 29-mile range SSN-10 system – for these missiles no external guidance was needed. With a new conformation of the foremast a *Top Sail* 3-D surveillance radar was fitted. Although, as with the previous cruisers, the "Kresta II's" Soviet designation is *Bolshoy Protivo Lodochny Korabl* (large anti-submarine ship) this class has an unrivalled all-round capability for a ship of her size. That the Soviet Navy realises this is shown by the fact that, despite the appearance of a new class, the eighth "Kresta II" is even now (1975) completing and more may be expected.

On 2 March 1973, the first ship of the new "Kara" class, *Nikolayev*, entered the Mediterranean from the Black Sea. She was much larger than the "Krestas" at 10,000 tons, carried the same eight SSN-10 launchers and two twin SAN-3s but also mounted four SAN-4 launchers for a new type of SAM missile. Her gunnery, however, was of greater power showing a return to a 76-mm main armament with four mountings for what appear to be 30-mm Gatling-type guns, as in the "Kresta II". A VDS sonar set added to her A/S capability and with gas turbines in place of steam machinery this class, which is now in series production, has given the USSR a new dimension in cruiser development. A decision on the form this class should take was probably reached in 1964 – two years after the debacle of Cuba and a year after Admiral Gorshkov had given his fleet the order to "get to sea".

CRUISERS

3 "Kara" Class (CLG)

Nikolayev
Ochakov
+*1*

Displacement, tons	8,200 standard; 10,000 full load
Length, feet (*metres*)	570 (*173·8*)
Beam, feet (*metres*)	60 (*18·3*)
Draught, feet (*metres*)	20 (*6·2*)
Aircraft	1 *Hormone*-A helicopter (hangar aft)
Missile Systems	8 SSN-10 (two mounts abreast bridge); 4 SAN-4 (twins either side of mast); 4 SAN-3 (twins for'd and aft)
Guns	4 76-mm (2 twins abaft bridge); 4 30-mm (abreast funnel) (see *Gunnery* note)

"Kara" class cruiser
Nikolayev

A/S weapons	2 16-barrelled MBU launchers (forward); 2 6-barrelled MBU launchers (aft)
Torpedo tubes	10 21-in (2 quintuple mountings abaft funnel)
Main engines	Gas-turbine
Speed, knots	Approximately 34

Apart from the specialised "Moskva" class this is the first large cruiser to join the Soviet Navy since the "Sverdlovs". Built at Nikolayev, she was first seen in public when she entered the Mediterranean from the Black Sea on 2 March 1973. Clearly capable of prolonged operations overseas.

ECM. A full outfit appears to be housed on the bridge and mast.

Missiles. In addition to the "Kresta II" armament of eight tubes for the SSN-10 (29-mile) surface-to-surface system and the pair of twin launchers for SAN-3 system with *Goblet* missiles, "Kara" mounts the new SAN-4 system in two silos, either side of the mast. The combination of such a number of systems presents a formidable capability, matched by no other ship.

Gunnery. The sighting of both main and secondary armament on either beams in the waist follows the precedent of both "Kresta" classes, although the weight of the main armament is increased. The single mountings, classified above as 30-mm, appear to be some form of Gatling and are quite different from the usual twin 30-mm mountings.

Radar. *Topsail* and *Headnet*-C; *Headlight* for SAN-3 system; *Owl Screech* for 76-mm guns; separate systems for SAN-4; *Drum Tilt* for 30-mm guns; *Pop Group* and *Don*.

Sonar and A/S. VDS is mounted below the helicopter pad and is presumably complementary to a hull-mounted set or sets. The presence of the helicopter with dipping-sonar and an A/S weapon load adds to her long-range capability.

Soviet Type Name. *Bolshoy Protivo Lodochny Korabl*, meaning Large Anti-Submarine Ship.

6 + 2 "Kresta II" Class (CLG)

Admiral Isakov
Admiral Makarov
Admiral Nakhimov
Admiral Oktyabrsky
Kronstadt
Marshal Voroshilov

Displacement, tons	6,000 standard; 8,000 full load
Length, feet (*metres*)	519·9 (*158·5*)
Beam, feet (*metres*)	55·1 (16·8)
Draught, feet (*metres*)	19·7 (*6·0*)
Aircraft	1 *Hormone*-A
Missile launchers	2 quadruple for SSN-10; 2 twin for SAN-3
A/S weapons	2 12-barrelled MBU forward and 2 6-barrelled MBU aft
Torpedo tubes	10 21-in (two quintuple)
Guns	4 57-mm (2 twin); 4 "Gatling" type
Main engines	Steam turbines; 2 shafts; 100,000 shp
Boilers	4 watertube
Speed, knots	33
Range, miles	5,000 at 18 knots
Complement	500

"Kresta II" class
cruiser *Admiral
Makarov*

"Kresta II" class

The design was developed from that of the "Kresta I" class, but the layout is more sophisticated. The missile armament shows an advance on the "Kresta I" SAM armament and a complete change of practice in the fitting of the SSN-10 system with 29-mile range missiles. This is a Mach 1·2 missile and the fact that it has subsequently been fitted in the "Kara" and "Krivak" classes indicates a possible change in tactical thought. Built at Leningrad from 1968 onwards, the first entering service in 1969.

Aircraft. A flight of two helicopters could be operated, although the normal would appear to be one on the apron aft with adjacent low hangar.

Gunnery. A new point-defence system is installed in four mounts, apparently of "Gatling" type.

New Construction. Two building at Zhdanov Yard Leningrad (1975).

Radar *Top Sail* 3-D and *Head Net*-C 3-D for search radar and the *Head Light* and *Peel Group* (2) fire control radar for surface-to-air missiles and *Drum Tilt* (2) for guns. *Muff Cob* and *Don* also fitted.

Soviet Type Name. *Bolshoy Protivo Lodochny Korabl*, meaning Large Anti-Submarine Ship.

4 "Kresta I" Class (CLG)

Vice-Admiral Drozd
Admiral Zozulya
Sevastopol
Vladivostok

Displacement, tons	6,140 standard; 8,000 full load
Length, feet (*metres*)	510 (*155·5*)
Beam, feet (*metres*)	55·1 (*16·8*)
Draught, feet (*metres*)	18·0 (*5·5*)
Aircraft	1 *Hormone*-A helicopter with hangar aft
Missile launchers	2 twin SSN-3 for *Shaddock* (no reloads); 2 twin SAN-1 for *Goa*
A/S weapons	2 12-barrelled MBU (60 reloads) forward; 2 6-barrelled MBU aft
Torpedo tubes	10 21-in (two quintuple)
Guns	4 57-mm (2 twin)
Main engines	Steam turbines; 2 shafts; 100,000 shp
Boilers	4 watertube
Speed, knots	34
Range, miles	4,500 at 18 knots
Complement	400

"Kresta I" class

Provided with a helicopter hangar and flight apron aft for the first time in a Soviet ship. This gives an enhanced A/S capability and could certainly provide carried-on-board target location facilities for the 400-mile SSN-3 system at a lower, possibly optimum, range of 100 miles. The "Kresta I" was therefore the first Soviet missile cruiser free to operate alone and distant from her own aircraft.

Built at the Zhdanov Shipyard, Leningrad. The prototype ship was laid down in September 1964, launched in 1965 and carried out sea-trials in the Baltic in February 1967. The second ship was launched in 1966 and the others in 1967–68.

Radar. Search: *Head Net*-C 3-D and *Big Net*. Fire Control: *Scoop Pair* for *Shaddock* system and *Peel Group* (2) for *Goa* systems. *Muff Cob*, *Don* and *Plinth Net*.

Soviet Type Name. *Bolshoy Protivo Lodochny Korabl*, meaning Large Anti-Submarine Ship.

4 "Kynda" Class (CLG)

Admiral Fokin
Admiral Golovko
Grozny
Varyag

"Kynda" class

Displacement, tons	4,500 standard; 6,000 full load
Length, feet (*metres*)	465·8 (*142·0*)
Beam, feet (*metres*)	51·8 (*15·8*)
Draught, feet (*metres*)	17·4 (*5·3*)
Aircraft	Pad for helicopter on stern
Missile launchers	2 quadruple mounts, 1 fwd, 1 aft, for SSN-3 system (possible reloads); 1 twin mount on forecastle for SAN-1 system (30 reloads)
A/S weapons	2 12-barrelled MBUs on forecastle
Guns, AA	4 3-in (*76*-mm) 2 twin
Torpedo tubes	6 21-in (*533*-mm) 2 triple ASW amidships
Main engines	2 sets geared turbines; 2 shafts; 100,000 shp
Boilers	4 high pressure
Speed, knots	35
Complement	390

The first ship of this class was laid down in June 1960, launched in April 1961 at Zhdanov Shipyard, Leningrad, and completed in June 1962. The second ship was launched in November 1961 and fitted out in August 1962. The others were completed by 1965. Two enclosed towers, instead of masts, are stepped forward of each raked funnel. In this class there is no helicopter embarked, so guidance for the SSN-3 system would be more difficult than in later ships. She will therefore be constrained in her operations compared with the "Kresta I" with her own helicopter.

Radar. This class showed at an early stage the Soviet ability to match radar availability to weapon capability. The duplicated aerials provide not only a capability for separate target engagement but also provide a reserve in the event of damage. Search: *Head Net*-A. Fire Control: *Scoop Pair* (2) for *Shaddock* systems, *Peel Group* for *Goa* systems and *Owl Screech* for gun, as well as *Don*.

Soviet Type Name. *Bolshoy Protivo Lodochny Korabl*, meaning Large Anti-Submarine Ship.

1 "Sverdlov" Class (CG)
2 "Sverdlov" Class (CC)
9 "Sverdlov" Class (CA)

Admiral Lazarev
Admiral Senyavin
Admiral Ushakov
Aleksandr Nevski
Aleksandr Suvorov
Dmitri Pozharski
Dzerzhinski
Mikhail Kutusov
Murmansk
Oktyabrskaya Revolutsiya
Sverdlov
Zhdanov

210m   18000t

Displacement, tons	15,450 standard; 18,000 full load
Length, feet (*metres*)	656·2 (*200·0*) pp; 689·0 (*210·0*) oa
Beam, feet (*metres*)	72·2 (*22·0*)
Draught, feet (*metres*)	24·5 (*7·5*)
Aircraft	Helicopter pad in *Zhdanov*. Pad and hangar in *Senyavin*
Armour	Belts 3·9–4·9 in (*100–125 mm*); fwd and aft 1·6–2 in (*40–50 mm*); turrets 4·9 in (*125 mm*); C.T. 5·9 in (*150 mm*); decks 1–2 in (*25–50 mm*) and 2–3 in (*50–75 mm*)
Missile launchers	Twin SAN-2 aft in *Dzerzhinski*; 2 SAN-4 in *Zhdanov* and *Senyavin* (twin)
Guns	12 6-in (*152-mm*), (4 triple) (9 6-in in *Dzerzhinski* and *Zhdanov*; 6 6-in in *Senyavin*) 12 3·9-in (*100-mm*), (6 twin) 32 37-mm (twin), 8 30-mm (16 twin)
Torpedo tubes	10 21-in (*533-mm*) 2 quintuple (see *Torpedoes*)
Mines	150 capacity (except *Zhdanov* and *Senyavin*)
Boilers	6 watertube
Main engines	Geared turbines; 2 shafts; 130,000 shp
Speed, knots	34
Range, miles	8,700 at 18 knots
Oil fuel, tons	3,800
Complement	1,000 average

"Sverdlov" class

This design is an improved "Chapaev", being the first post-war class of cruisers laid down. Of the twenty-four originally projected, twenty keels were laid and seventeen hulls were launched from 1951 onwards, but only fourteen ships were completed by 1956. There were two slightly different types. The original ships had the 37-mm AA guns near the fore-funnel one deck higher than in later cruisers. All ships except *Zhdanov* and *Senyavin* are fitted for minelaying. Mine stowage is on the second deck. *Zhdanov* and *Senyavin* used as command ships with much increased communications capability. *Admiral Nakhimov* deleted in 1969.

Dzerzhinski has been fitted with an SAN-2 launcher aft replacing X-Turret. In 1972 *Admiral Senyavin* returned to service with both X and Y turrets removed and replaced by a helicopter pad and a hangar surmounted by 4 30-mm mountings and an SAN-4 mounting. At about the same time *Zhdanov* appeared on the scene with a different outfit. She has had only X-turret removed and replaced by a high deckhouse mounting an SAN-4 launcher.

Names. The ship first named *Molotovsk* was renamed *Oktyabrskaya Revolutsiya* in 1957.

Radar. *Neptun, High Sieve, Big Net, Knife Rest, Top Trough, Top Bow, Hair Net, Sun Visor, Egg Cup*. Outfits vary in different ships. *Fan Song*-E and *High Lune* in *Dzerzhinski*.

Torpedoes. *Oktyabrskaya Revolutsiya* and *Murmansk* no longer have tubes.

Soviet Type Name. *Kreyser*, meaning Cruiser.

Zhdanov

Komsomolets (ex-Chklov)
Zheleznyakov

2 "Chapaev" Class (CA)

Displacement, tons	11,300 standard; 15,000 full load
Length, feet (*metres*)	659·5 (*201·0*) wl; 665 (*202·8*) oa
Beam, feet (*metres*)	62 (*18·9*)
Draught, feet (*metres*)	24 (*7·3*)
Guns	12 6-in (*152-mm*) 57 cal, (4 triple); 8 3·9-in (*100-mm*) 70 cal, (4 twin); 24 37-mm (12 twin)
Mines	200 capacity; 425-ft rails
Boilers	6 watertube
Main engines	Geared turbines, with diesels for cruising speeds; 4 shafts; 130,000 shp
Speed, knots	32
Range, miles	5,400 at 15 knots
Oil fuel, tons	2,500
Complement	900

Originally a class of six ships of the "Chapaev" or "Frunze" class of which one was never completed – show signs of both Italian and German influence. Launched during 1941–47. All work on these ships was stopped during the war, but was resumed in 1946–47. Completed in 1948–50 both in Leningrad. Catapults were removed from all ships of this type. Both remaining ships serve as training cruisers.

Gunnery. Turret guns fitting allows independent elevation to 50 degrees.

Radar. *Neptun, Low Sieve, Slim Net, Top Bow, Sun Visor, Egg Cup.*

"Chapaev" class
cruiser *Komsomolets*

Soviet Type Name. *Kreyser*, meaning Cruiser.

Destroyers

When the First World War was exchanged for the equally sanguinary struggles of the Revolution and its resultant hostilities the Russian destroyer force was of considerable size. Pride of place was given to *Novik* of 1,262 tons and 36 knots – in 1914 an additional thirty-six of this class were planned but very few were built. In 1924 of the fifteen destroyers listed five were of this class and they had been sufficiently successful for the first post-war design to be for a large (2,580 tons), fast (36 knots) class, the "Leningrads". Although their construction in the mid-1930s was supervised by French experts, the design was poor and they turned out to be bad sea boats. Further outside assistance was called in, this time from Italy. The 3,200-ton *Tashkent* was designed and built at Livorno and on trials, before her guns were fitted, achieved 45.8 knots with 110,000 shp. The pattern of large, fast ships was continued with the "Kiev" class, none of which was, however, ever completed though four were under construction when war broke out in 1941.

Classes of smaller ships had been completed in dribs and drabs in the years between the wars so that by mid-1941 the total was in the region of 70–80 with a number of torpedo-boats in addition. At the war's end, including Lend/Lease ships, the few completed in the previous four years and some captured vessels, the total was down to fifty-two. This was a motley outfit, ill-provided with sensors and modern armament and manned, on the whole, by incompetent ships' companies. But some which survived were of a higher standard than the rest, although equally deficient in sensors until Allied stores were fitted. These were the surviving twenty-five ships of the forty-six "Gordy" and "Silny" classes of 2,000 and 2,250 tons respectively. They were handsome ships as befitted the Italian interest in their original design but the "Gordys" were not good sea boats. Greater attention was paid to this in the "Ognevoy" class, the first Soviet destroyers designed with twin turrets for their four 5.1-inch (130-mm) guns. Some ten of these pre-war designed ships were completed after the war, joining the dozen or so ships of the "Ryany" and "Vnimatelny" classes which were slightly smaller.

In 1949 came the first of the new post-war designed "Skory" class –

3,100 tons and 38 knots with two twin 5.1-inch turrets. It is believed that eighty-five of these were planned for Stalin's new fleet but only seventy were completed. Close on their heels came the "Tallin" class of a larger size and with an imposing tower foremast carrying the stabilised director. The first of these four ships appeared in 1954 and they were followed a year later by the lead-ship of the "Kotlin" class. These were conventional destroyers armed with 5.1-inch guns and using similar hull-design and machinery to the "Tallins". Forty of these were planned but, in the event, four hulls were converted into "Kildin" class carrying the Soviet's first seaborne surface-to-surface missile system, the SSN-1, and eight became "SAM Kotlin" conversions with a twin SAN-1 launcher aft.

It is at this period that the flexibility of Soviet naval architects' planning becomes clear. From "Tallin" to "Kotlin", from "Kotlin" to "Kildin" and "SAM Kotlin" – all with similar hull and machinery, but with swift reaction to improvements in weapon systems and frequently using equipment earmarked for other classes which were cancelled or modified. While the four "Kildins" were being converted to carry a single SSN-1 the larger "Krupny" class (4,650 tons) was started in 1958 (completing two years later), the last class to be fitted with the SSN-1 system. These were probably also converted in the design stage from all-gun successors to the "Kotlin" with modern AA and A/S systems. Once again the full planned total was not completed – only eight were built of which seven have been converted to "Kanins" since 1967. This alteration was a major one – the SSN-1 was replaced by a twin SAN-1 and the A/S capability was much improved, probably by taking up equipment from yet another cancelled order. A pattern of specialisation in either surface-to-surface or surface-to-air missile systems had now emerged and from the "Krupnys" onwards for the next ten years surface-to-surface missiles were concentrated in the cruisers. This specialisation was clear in the 1962 "Kashin" class of 4,500 tons with two twin SAN-1 mountings, a considerable A/S potential and the first major warships in the world with an all gas-turbine propulsion system. This appears to have been part of an integrated plan by which the destroyers provided the AA protection for the SSM cruisers, both having their own A/S protection.

Then in 1971 the first of the "Krivak" class appeared, a thousand tons less than the "Kashins" but armed with the new SSN-10 surface to-surface missiles with a range of about 25 miles and two twin launchers for the new SAN-4 point defence missile system. With VDS as well as a chin-mounted sonar, two 12-barrelled MBUs and eight 21-inch torpedo-tubes her A/S potential was well up to standard, although, as mentioned in the sections on A/S weapons, it is still surprising that no long-range missile for this purpose has yet appeared. It is just possible that a hitherto unidentified weapon may be available for firing in place of one of the other missiles. However this may turn out, the facts are simple – nine "Krivaks" are available and this handsome, handy and well-armed destroyer is in series production.

9 "Krivak" Class (DDG)

Bditelny
Bodry
Doblestny
Dostoyny
Silny
Storozhevoy
Svirepy
+2

Displacement, tons	3,500 standard; 4,200 full load
Length, feet (*metres*)	404·8 (*123·4*)
Beam, feet (*metres*)	45·9 (*14·0*)
Draught, feet (*metres*)	16·4 (*5·0*)
Missile launchers	4 for SSN-10 system, in "A" position; (quadruple); 2 for SAN-4 system (twins)
Guns	4 3-in (*76-mm*) dual-purpose automatic (2 twin) in "X" and "Y" positions; 4 30-mm
A/S weapons	2 12-barrelled MBUs forward in "B" position
Torpedo tubes	8 21-in (*533-mm*) in two quadruple banks on either side amidships
Main engines	8 sets Gas turbines; 2 shafts; 112,000 shp
Speed, knots	38

Two views of the "Krivak" class destroyer

This handsome class, the first ship of which appeared in 1971, appears to be a most successful design incorporating surface and anti-air capability, a VDS with associated MBUs, two banks of tubes, all in a hull designed for both speed and sea-keeping. The use of gas-turbines gives the "Krivak" class a rapid acceleration and an availability which cannot be matched by steam-driven ships. Building continues at about two per year.

Missiles. The surface-to-surface missiles of the SSN-10 system have a range of 29 miles, continuing the short-range trend of the "Kresta II" class and followed by the "Kara" class. The SAN-4 SAMs are of a new design which is now mounted also in the "Kuril", "Kara", "Nanuchka" and "Grisha" classes. The launcher retracts into the mounting for stowage and protection, rising to fire and retracting to reload. The two mountings are forward of the bridge and abaft the funnel.

Radar. *Head Net*-C, *Pop Group*, *Owl Screech*, *Don*.

Soviet Type Name. *Bolshoy Protivo Lodochny Korabl*, meaning Large Anti-Submarine Ship.

19 "Kashin" and "Modified Kashin" Class (DDG)

KASHIN

MOD KASHIN

Displacement, tons	3,750 standard; 4,500 (4,700 modified) full load
Length, feet (*metres*)	470·9 (*143·3*) or 481 (*146·5*)
Beam, feet (*metres*)	52·5 (*15·9*)
Draught, feet (*metres*)	19 (*5·8*)
Missile launchers	4 (2 twin) SAN-1 mounted in "B" and "X" positions for surface-to-air missiles; 4 SSN-11 in mod-class
Guns	4 3-in (*76-mm*), 2 twin, in "A" and "Y" positions; 4 30-mm Gatlings in mod. class
A/S weapons	2 12-barrelled MBU forward; 2 6-barrelled MBU aft
Torpedo tubes	5 21-in (*533-mm*) quintuple, amidships for ASW torpedoes

Main engines	8 sets gas turbines; each 12,000 hp; 2 shafts; 96,000 shp	"Modified Kashin" class
Speed, knots	35	
Complement	350	

The first class of warships in the world to rely entirely on gas-turbine propulsion giving them the quick getaway and acceleration necessary for modern tactics. These ships were delivered from 1962 onwards from the Zhdanov Yard, Leningrad and the Nosenko Yard, Nikolayev.

This class, although comparatively youthful, have been outdated by recent building. Lacking SSM, a modern SAM system and VDS they were in line for modernisation. This has now started – the conversion consists of a hull-lengthening by ten feet, the shipping of 4 SSN-11 SSM launchers, 4 30-mm Gatling guns, a VDS and MBU 4500 launchers.

One of this class foundered in the Black Sea in September 1974, apparently as the result of an internal explosion followed by a fire which lasted for five hours. Nearly 300 of the ship's company were lost, making this the worst peacetime naval loss for many years.

Radar. Search: *Head Net*-C and *Big Net* in some ships; *Head Net*-A (2) in others. Fire control: *Peel Group* (2) for Goa systems and *Owl Screech* (2) for guns. *Don.*

Soviet Type Name. *Bolshoy Protivo Lodochny Korabl*, meaning Large Anti-Submarine Ship.

4 "Kildin" Class (DDG)

Bedovy
Neudersimy
Neulovimy
Prozorlivy

KILDIN

111

MOD KILDIN

Displacement, tons	3,000 standard; 3,600 full load
Length, feet (*metres*)	414·9 (*126·5*)
Beam, feet (*metres*)	42·6 (*13·0*)
Draught, feet (*metres*)	16·1 (*4·9*)
Missile launchers	4 for SSN-11 system
A/S weapons	2 16-in barrelled MBU on forecastle
Guns	4 76-mm (twins aft); 16 57-mm (quads, 2 forward, 2 between funnels)
Torpedo tubes	4 21-in (2 twin)
Main engines	Geared turbines; 2 shafts; 72,000 shp
Boilers	4 high pressure
Speed, knots	36
Range, miles	5,500 at 16 knots
Complement	350

This class used the Kotlin-type hull and machinery but were originally armed with a single SSN-1 launcher aft. *Bedovy* mounted 16 45-mm guns, the remainder 16 57-mm. Building dates 1957–60 at Nikolayev and Zhdarov Yards.

In 1972 *Neulovimy* was taken in hand for modification. This was completed in mid-1973 and consisted of the replacement of the SSN-1 on the quarterdeck by 2 superimposed twin 76-mm turrets, the fitting of 4 SSN-11 launchers abreast the after funnel and the fitting of new radar. The substitution of the 29-mile SSN-11 system (a modified *Styx*) for the obsolescent SSN-1 system and the notable increase in gun armament illustrate two trends in Soviet thought. A second ship of the class has now completed this conversion and the other pair are in hand.

Radar. Search: *Head Net*-A and *Slim Net*. Fire Control: New outfit at modernisation.

Soviet Type Name. Rated *Bolshoy Protivo Lodochny Kerabl*, meaning Large Anti-Submarine Ship.

"Modified Kildin" class destroyer *Neulovimy*

7 "Kanin" Class (DDG)

Boyky
Derzky
Gnevny
Gremyashchyi
Zhguchy
Zorky
+ *I*

Displacement, tons	3,700 standard; 4,700 full load
Length, feet (*metres*)	456.9 (*139·3*)
Beam, feet (*metres*)	48·2 (*14·7*)
Draught, feet (*metres*)	16·4 (*5·0*)
Aircraft	Helicopter pad
Missile launchers	1 twin SAN-1 mounted aft
A/S weapons	3 12-barrelled MBU
Guns	8 57-mm (2 quadruple forward); 8 30-mm (twin) (by after funnel)
Torpedo tubes	10 21-in (*533*-mm) A/S (2 quintuple)
Main engines	2 sets geared steam turbines, 2 shafts; 80,000 shp
Boilers	4 watertube
Oil fuel, tons	900
Speed, knots	34
Complement	350

All ships of this class have been converted from "Krupnys" at Zhdanov Yard, Leningrad from 1967 onwards, being given a SAM capability instead of the latter's SSM armament. As compared with the "Krupny" class these ships have enlarged bridge, converted bow, (probably for a new sonar) and larger helicopter platforms.

"Kanin" class

"Kanin" class
destroyer *Boyky*.

Gunnery. The 4 twin 30-mm abaft the after funnel were a late addition to the armament.

Radar. Search: *Head Net*-C or *Head Net*-A. Fire Control: *Peel Group* for *Goa* systems, *Hawk Screech* for guns. *Drum Tilt* for additional 30-mm guns. *Don.*

Soviet Type Name. *Bolshoy Protivo Lodochny Korabl*, meaning Large Anti-Submarine Ship.

Gordy

1 "Krupny" Class (DDG)

Displacement, tons	3,650 standard; 4,650 full load
Length, feet (*metres*)	452 (*137·8*)
Beam, feet (*metres*)	48·2 (*14·7*)
Draught, feet (*metres*)	16·5 (*5·0*)
Missile launchers	2 mountings; 1 forward, 1 aft for SSN-1 system
Guns	16 57-mm (4 quadruple)
A/S weapons	2 16-barrelled MBUs
Torpedo launchers	6 (2 triple) for 21-in A/S torpedoes
Main engines	Geared steam turbines; 2 shafts; 80,000 shp
Boilers	4 high-pressure water tube
Speed, knots	34
Complement	360

This class was probably originally designed as all-gun destroyers to be the Kotlins' successors. However they were converted to carry SSN-1 launches at both ends with a helicopter pad on the quarter-deck. Initial construction started in 1958 at Leningrad. Four ships of this class were converted to carry surface-to-air missiles in 1967 to 1971 and are known as the "Kanin" class; three more subsequently converted.

"Krupny" class

Radar. Search: *Head Net*-A. Fire Control: *Hawk Screech* (2), *Top Bow*, *Neptun*.

Soviet Type Name. Rated as *Raketny Korabl*, meaning Rocket Ship

8 "Sam Kotlin" Class (DDG)

Bravy
Nakhodchivy
Nastoychivy
Nesokrushimy
Skromny
Skrytny
Soznatelny
Vozbuzhdenny

115

"SAM Kotlin" class

Displacement, tons	2,850 standard; 3,600 full load
Length, feet (*metres*)	414·9 (*126·5*)
Beam, feet (*metres*)	42·6 (*13·0*)
Draught, feet (*metres*)	16·1 (*4·9*)
Missile launchers	1 twin SAN-1 mounted aft (20 missiles)
Guns	2 5·1-in (*130-mm*) dp (1 twin); 2 or 4 57-mm AA (1 twin or quadruple); 8 30-mm in some
Torpedo tubes	1 quintuple 21-in mounting
A/S weapons	6 side-thrown DC projectors or 2 12-barrelled MBU rocket launchers
Main engines	Geared turbines; 2 shafts; 72,000 shp
Boilers	4 high pressure
Speed, knots	36
Range, miles	5,500 at 16 knots
Complement	285

Converted "Kotlin" class destroyers with a surface-to-air missile launcher in place of the 5·1-in twin turret aft and anti-aircraft guns reduced to a single 57-mm mounting forward. Some recently fitted with eight 30-mm. The prototype "SAM Kotlin" class has a different after funnel and different radar pedestal from those in the standard "SAM Kotlin" class.

The prototype conversion was completed about 1962 and the others since 1966. One ship transferred to Poland.

Radar. Search: *Head Net*-C. Fire Control: *Peel Group* for *Goa* systems, *Hawk Screech* for guns. *Drum Tilt* for 30-mm in later ships. *Egg Cup*, *Sun Visor* and *Don*.

Soviet Type Name. *Esminets*, meaning Destroyer.

18 "Kotlin" Class (DD)

Bessledny
Blagorodny
Blestyashchy
Burlivy
Syvaly
Naporisty
Plamenny
Speshny
Dalnevostochny
   Komsomolets
Moskovsky Komsomolets
Spokojny
Spravedlivy
Svetly
Vdokhnovenny
Vozmushchenny
Vyderzhanny
+2

Displacement, tons	2,850 standard; 3,600 full load
Length, feet (*metres*)	414·9 (*126·5*)
Beam, feet (*metres*)	42·6 (*13·0*)
Draught, feet (*metres*)	16·1 (*4·9*)
Guns	4 5·1-in (*130-mm*) (2 twin); 16 45-mm AA (4 quadruple); (8 30-mm in some)
A/S weapons	6 side-thrown DC projectors or (2 16-barrelled MBUs in some)
Torpedo tubes	10 21-in (*533-mm*) (5 only in some)
Mines	80 capacity
Main engines	Geared turbines; 2 shafts; 72,000 shp
Boilers	4 high pressure
Speed, knots	36
Range, miles	5,500 at 16 knots
Complement	285

Built in 1954–57. The last four hulls laid down were converted to "Kildins". Eight were converted to "SAM Kotlin" plus one transferred to Poland. *Svetly* and others were provided with helicopter pad on stern. Some had the after torpedo-tubes replaced by a deckhouse. Some ships also had 2 16-barrelled MBUs fitted while the latest addition in some ships is the fitting of 8 30-mm either side of the after-funnel.

Radar. Search: *Slim New*. Fire Control: *Hawk Screech* (2). *Sun Visor, Egg Cup, Don* or *Neptun*.

Soviet Type Name. *Esminets*, meaning Destroyer.

Modified "Kotlin" class

40 "Skory" Class (DD)

SKORY

MOD SKORY

Displacement, tons	2,600 standard; 3,100 full load
Length, feet (*metres*)	395·2 (*120·5*)
Beam, feet (*metres*)	38·9 (*11·8*)
Draught, feet (*metres*)	15·1 (*4·6*)
Guns	4 5·1-in (*130-mm*), 2 twin; 2 3·4-in (*85-mm*) 1 twin 8 37-mm (4 twin) (*see notes*)
A/S weapons	4 DCT (*see notes*)
Torpedo tubes	10 21-in (*533-mm*) (*see notes*)
Mines	80 can be carried
Main engines	Geared turbines; 2 shafts; 60,000 shp
Boilers	4 high pressure
Speed, knots	33
Range, miles	3,900 at 13 knots
Complement	260

There were to have been eighty-five destroyers of this class, but construction beyond seventy units was discontinued in favour of later types of destroyers, and the number has been further reduced to forty by transfers to other types and disposals at an increasing rate. First appeared in 1949.

There were three differing types in this class, the anti-aircraft guns varying with twin and single mountings; and two types of foremast, one vertical with all scanners on top and the other with one scanner on top and one on a platform half way. At least six ships, of the "Skory" class were modified from 1959 onwards including extensive alterations to anti-aircraft armament, electronic equipment and anti-submarine weapons. These now have 5 57-mm single, 5 torpedo tubes and 2 16-barrelled MBUs.

Radar. Modernised: *Hawk Screech, Slim Net* and *Don*. Original: *Cross-Bird* or *Knife Rest*.

"Modified Skory" class
destroyer *Ognenny*

1 "Tallin" Class (DD)

Neustrashimy

Displacement, tons	3,200 standard; 4,300 full load
Length, feet (*metres*)	440·0 (*134·0*) oa
Beam, feet (*metres*)	44·9 (*13·7*)
Draught, feet (*metres*)	16·1 (*4·9*)
Guns	4 5·1-in (*130-mm*) semi-automatic (2 twin); 16 57-mm (4 quadruple)
A/S weapons	2 16-barrelled MBUs and 2 DC launchers
Torpedo tubes	10 21-in (*533-mm*), 2 quintuple
Mines	70
Main engines	Geared turbines; 2 shafts; 80,000 shp
Boilers	4 water tube
Speed, knots	38
Range, miles	2,500 at 18 knots
Oil fuel, tons	850
Complement	340

Last of a class of four, built in 1952–54 as a larger follow-on class to the
"Skorys".

Gunnery. The 5·1-in (*130-mm*) guns in 2 twin turrets, including the
directors, are fully stabilised.

Radar. Search: *Slim Net*. Fire Control: *Hawk Screech* (2). *Knife Rest,
Sun Visor, Egg Cup* and *Don*.

Soviet Type Name. *Esminets*, meaning Destroyer.

Frigates and Corvettes

Despite the various classifications used by the Soviet navy, such as Escort ship and Small Anti-Submarine Ship, the two classifications given above are used in this book. A "frigate" is taken as a surface ship of 1,100 to 3,000 tons excepting the original conventional destroyers, and a "corvette" as 500 to 1,100 tons.

Ships of these classifications can really be dealt with only in the post-1945 period, although a very mixed bag of approximately frigate–corvette size were listed in 1939. The first post-war class to appear was the "Kola" class of which twenty-four were completed between 1950–52. These were akin to the "Gordy" destroyers in appearance and the arrangement of their four 3·9-inch (100-mm) guns in single mountings and just topped the 1,900-ton mark with a speed of 30 knots. Barely were they in commission than the "Rigas" appeared, probably a contemporary in the drawing office to the "Skorys". Smaller (1,600 tons) than the "Kolas" and slower (28 knots) they provided little advance, although in later years the survivors of the original class of seventy have been modified to carry MBU A/S weapons and, in the last few years, extra 30-mm guns.

After the end of the "Riga" building programme in 1959 there was a halt of about a couple of years before the first "Petya" appeared in 1961. The size was again reduced, this time to 1,150 tons but the combination of gas-turbines and diesels gave her an increase of speed to 33 knots and, presumably, an increase in range. The gas-turbine, also used in the contemporary "Kashins", had come to stay. The gun armament was reduced to 3-inch (76-mm) but the A/S armament in the first group was increased to four MBUs and five torpedo tubes but this was reversed in the "Petya IIs" to two MBUs and ten tubes, an interesting view of the rival merits of the A/S torpedo and the 16-barrelled MBU. Twenty "Petya Is" and twenty-five "Petya IIs" were completed in 1961–63 being followed in 1964 by the first of the "Mirka" class which also had two variants, "I" and "II", with the same alterations in armament as the "Petyas". The layout of the propulsion plant was different in "Mirka" from "Petya" but the result was much the same. Some of both classes have been fitted with VDS. Twenty "Mirkas" were completed between 1964–69.

The three classes of corvettes which followed the war, "Kronstadt" (1948–56) of which some 230 were built, "SO I" (1957–61) of which round about 100 were built and "Poti" (1961–68) with seventy units were of varying sizes and differing propulsion plants.

The "Kronstadts" were of a basic war-time design whilst the "SO I", smaller by over 100 tons than their 380-ton predecessors, were five knots faster at 29 knots. The "Potis" reversed the trend towards smaller ships, being of 600 tons, a size probably dictated by their new propulsion layout. In addition to the "SO I"'s diesels they were fitted with a pair of gas-turbines although the speed was apparently unaffected, unlike the notable increase achieved in their contemporaries, the "Petyas". The additional size allowed for the mounting of larger (57-mm) guns and MBUs as well as the fitting of a quadruple 16-inch torpedo tube mounting. In fact the "Poti" is, by the definitions used in this book, the only one of these three classes which is a true "corvette" – the other pair has been included in this section in view of their employment in the Soviet fleet.

After the completion of the last of the "Potis" in 1968 there was a short gap before the next class appeared, the "Nanuchka" class, which is a true corvette in many respects. In some ways comparison with the "Petya/Mirka" classes is of interest, in others these ships must be considered as a development of the "Osas". The first of the "Nanuchkas" appeared in 1969, at 850 tons half-way in size between a "Poti" and a "Mirka". But her armament was very different; two triple launchers for the new SSN-9 missiles with a maximum range around 150 miles and a twin SAN-4 launcher forward put the "Nanuchka" in a completely different league. Twin 57-mm guns and MBUs when added to her missiles made this a formidable fighting ship whose larger size and 5:1 length/beam ratio meant an increased efficiency as a weapons platform in heavy weather. Despite the fact that gas-turbines had been at sea for at least seven years when she appeared diesels were preferred for her power-plant, as in the "Osas". Whether the experiments with gas-turbines in the "P8" and "P10" classes had been sufficiently unsucessful for the designers to consider them as best suited to ships in which there was more space is not known. The length of the "Potis" is about the same as "Nanuchka" but space below decks is presumably greater in view of the very different armament and this may be a reason for adopting the diesel-engine in the latter. Another possible reason is a difference in role between "Nanuchka", the strike-craft and the other corvettes, including the later "Grishas", which have a primary A/S role requiring the sharp acceleration given by gas-turbines. Whatever the background the new class is capable of over 30 knots and, as the building rate is about three a year, pose yet another considerable element of uncertainty for an opposed fleet commander. It is of interest that in the large Soviet fleet which gathered in the East Mediterranean at the time of the Yom Kippur war in October–November 1973 two "Nanuchkas" were included.

Last of this group is the "Grisha" class which has been seen since

1969–70 and is in production at the rate of about four a year. This class at 750 tons is presumably the true successor of the "Potis" and has the same armament as her predecessor with the addition, in the earlier ships of the class, of an SAN-4 launcher forward. Once again both diesels and gas-turbines are fitted, giving the good cruising radius and high burst-speed, up to 30 knots plus, required in A/S operations. In certain ships, the "Grisha II" class, the SAN-4 has been replaced by a second twin-57-mm mounting forward. The reason for this is again not clear. It could be a matter of space or of role or just doubts about the efficiency of the SAN-4 in a ship of these dimensions. Her length/beam ratio is 7 : 1 which might be causing behaviour problems but this is pure speculation.

What is not speculation is that the Soviet fleet is adding to its already notable strength in these smaller ships a continuing programme of specialised vessels with considerable potential in sea-keeping qualities, armament and speed. At the same time the majority of Western navies, although a number of commercial designs are available, have not, with the exception of the French with the A69/70 avisos, embarked on similar programmes.

FRIGATES

20 "Mirka I and II" Class

MIRKA II

Displacement, tons	950 standard; 1,100 full load
Length, feet (*metres*)	269·9 (*82·3*)
Beam, feet (*metres*)	29·9 (*9·1*)
Draught, feet (*metres*)	9·8 (*3·0*)
Guns	4 3-in (*76-mm*) (2 twin) (I)
A/S weapons	4 12-barrelled MBUs (2 forward, 2 aft) (I); 2 16-barrelled MBUs (II)
Torpedo tubes	5 16-in anti-submarine (I) 10 16-in (II)
Main engines	2 diesels; total 6,000 hp; 2 gas-turbines, total 31,000 hp; 2 shafts
Speed, knots	33
Complement	100

"Mirka II" class

This class of ships was built in 1964–69 as improved "Petya" class. With the removal of the funnel and the mast moved further aft the silhouettes of the two classes is quite different. The difference between the Mark I and II is that the latter have the after MBU rocket launchers removed and an additional quintuple 16-inch torpedo mounting fitted between the bridge and the mast. At least one mounts VDS aft.

Radar. Search: *Slim Net*. Fire Control: *Hawk Screech* and *Don*.

Soviet Type Name. *Storozhevoy Korabl*, meaning Escort Ship.

20 "Petya I" Class
25 "Petya II" Class

PETYA II

Displacement, tons	950 standard; 1,150 full load
Length, feet (*metres*)	270 (*82·3*)
Beam, feet (*metres*)	29·9 (*9·1*)
Draught, feet (*metres*)	10·5 (*3·2*)
Guns	4 3-in (*76-mm*) (2 twin)
A/S weapons	4 16-barrelled MBUs (I); 2 12-barrelled MBUs (II)
Torpedo tubes	5 16-in (*406-mm*) (I); 10 16-in (*406-mm*) (II)
Main engines	2 diesels, total 6,000 hp; 2 gas-turbines; total 30,000 hp; 2 shafts
Speed, knots	30
Complement	100

The first ship reported to have been built in 1960–61 at Kaliningrad. Construction continued until about 1964. Fitted with two mine rails. "Petya IIs" sacrifice MBUs for extra tubes whilst some of both classes have lost the after 3-in turret to compensate for VDS.

Radar. Search: *Slim Net.* Fire Control: *Hawk Screech; Neptun* or *Don.*

Soviet Type Name. *Storozhevoy Korabl,* meaning Escort Ship.

Left: "Petya I" class.
Below: "Petya II"
class (*US Navy*)

40 "Riga" Class

Barsuk
Bujvol
Byk
Gepard
Giena
Kobchik
Lev
Lisa
Medved
Pantera
Sakal
Tigr
Turman
Volk
+26

Displacement, tons	1,200 standard; 1,600 full load
Length, feet (*metres*)	298·8 (*91·0*)
Beam, feet (*metres*)	33·7 (*10·2*)
Draught, feet (*metres*)	11 (*3·4*)
Guns	3 3·9-in (*100-mm*) single; 4 37-mm (2 twin); 4 30-mm (twin) in some
A/S weapons	2 16-barrelled MBUs (in some); 4 DC projectors
Torpedo tubes	3 21-in (*533-mm*) (2 (twin) in some)
Mines	50
Main engines	Geared turbines; 2 shafts; 25,000 shp
Boilers	2
Speed, knots	28
Range, miles	2,500 at 15 knots
Complement	150

Two views of a "Riga" class frigate

Built from 1952 to 1959 – originally a class of seventy. Successors to the "Kola" class escorts, of which they are lighter and less heavily armed but improved versions. Fitted with mine rails.

A small number of this class has been converted. Some, designed for ECM operations, have a higher funnel, more complex electronics, no torpedo tubes but with MBU (A/S) launchers. Others have had the triple torpedo-tube mountings replaced by more modern twin mountings and have a twin 30-mm gun mounting on either side of the funnel.

Anti-Submarine. The two 16-barrelled MBU rocket launchers are mounted just before the bridge abreast "B" gun.

Radar. Search: *Slim Net. Sun Visor, Neptun* or *Don.*

Soviet Type Name. *Storozhevoy Korabl*, meaning Escort Ship.

Transfers. Bulgaria (2), China (4), East Germany (2), Finland (2), Indonesia (6).

"Riga" class

6 "Kola" Class

Doblestny
Sovietsky Azerbaidjan
Sovietsky Dagestan
Sovietsky Turkmenistan
Zesky
Zivuchi

Displacement, tons	1,500 standard; 1,900 full load
Length, feet (*metres*)	315·0 (*96·0*) oa
Beam, feet (*metres*)	35·4 (*10·8*)
Draught, feet (*metres*)	10·6 (*3·2*)
Guns	4 3·9-in (*100-mm*) single; 4 37-mm (twin)
A/S weapons	2 MBU; 4 DC racks; 4 DC rails
Torpedo tubes	3 21-in (*533-mm*)
Mines	30
Main engines	Geared turbines; 2 shafts; 30,000 shp
Boilers	2
Speed, knots	30
Range, miles	3,500 at 12 knots
Complement	190

Built in 1950–52 – originally a class of twenty-four. Three are stationed in the Caspian Sea, one is in reserve in the Baltic whilst two have been converted as auxiliaries.
Radar. Surface Search: *Ball Gun/Ball End*. Air Search: *Cross Bird*. Fire control: *Wasp Head* and *Sun Visor*. IFF: *High Pole*.

Soviet Type Name. *Storozhevoy Korabl*, meaning Escort Ship.

CORVETTES

17 "Grisha I" and "Grisha II" Classes

"Grisha II" class

Displacement, tons	900 full load
Dimensions, feet (*metres*)	234·8 × 32·8 × 9·2 (*71·6 × 10 × 2·8*)
Missile launchers	SAN-4 surface-to-air (twin) ("Grisha I" class)
Guns	2 57-mm dual purpose (1 twin) (4 in "Grisha II" class)
Torpedo tubes	4 16-in anti-submarine
A/S weapons	2 12-barrelled MBUs
Main engines	2 gas-turbines; 2 diesels
Speed, knots	30

Reported to have started series production in the late 1969–70 period. Five built by end of 1972, with a continuing programme of four a year. SAN-4 launcher mounted on the forecastle in "Grisha I" class. This is replaced by a second twin 57-mm in "Grisha II" class. See difference between silhouette and photograph.

Radar. *Strut Curve, Muff Cob, Pop Group* and *Don* in "Grisha I" class.

Soviet Type Name. *Maly Protivo Lodochny Korabl*, meaning Small Anti-Submarine Ship.

12 "Nanuchka" Class
(Missile Corvette)

Displacement, tons	800 normal (approx)
Dimensions, feet (*metres*)	196·8 × 39·6 × 9·9 (*60·0 × 12·0 × 3·0*)
Missile launchers	6 (2 triple) for SSN-9 surface-to-surface system; SAN-4 surface-to-air system forward (twin)
Guns	2 57-mm AA (1 twin)
A/S weapons	1 or 2 MBUs
Main engines	4 Diesels; 20,000 shp; 2 shafts
Speed, knots	30

A new class of diesel-powered craft with SSM launchers as the main armament. Probably mainly intended for deployment in coastal waters. The high beam-to-length ratio in a ship of this size should improve her steadiness as a firing platform. Built from 1969 onwards. Has received many type designations including "Missile Cutter". Building continues at rate of about three a year at Leningrad.

Radar. *Muff Cob, Pop Group, Don.*

"Nanuchka" class
(S. Breyer)

70 "POTI" Class

This class of ships was under series construction from 1961 to 1968.

Radar. *Strut Curve, Muff Cob* and *Don.*

Soviet Type Name. *Maly Protivo Lodochny Korabl*, meaning Small Anti-Submarine Ship.

Displacement, tons	550 standard; 600 full load
Dimensions, feet (*metres*)	193·5 × 26·2 × 9·2 (*59·0 × 8·0 × 2·8*)
Guns	2 57-mm AA (1 twin mounting)
Tubes	4 16-in anti-submarine
A/S weapons	2 12-barrelled MBUs
Main engines	2 gas turbines; 2 diesels; 4 shafts; total 20,000 hp
Speed, knots	28

80 "So I" Class

Displacement, tons	215 light; 250 normal
Dimensions, feet (*metres*)	138·6 × 20·0 × 9·2 (*42·3 × 6·1 × 2·8*)
Guns	4 25-mm AA (2 twin mountings)
A/S weapons	4 5-barrelled MBUs
Main engines	3 diesels; 6,000 bhp
Speed, knots	29
Range, miles	1,100 at 13 knots
Complement	30

Built since 1957. Steel-hulled. Modernised boats of this class have only two 25-mm AA guns but also have four 16-inch anti-submarine torpedo tubes. Being phased out of service.

Radar. *Pot Head.*

Soviet Type Name. *Maly Protivo Lodochny Korabl*, meaning Small Anti-Submarine Ship.

"Poti" class *(S. Breyer)*

"SO I" class

17 "Kronstradt" Class

Displacement, tons	310 standard; 380 full load
Dimensions, feet *(metres)*	170·6 × 21·5 × 9·0 *(52·0 × 6·6 × 2·7)*
Guns	1 3·5-in; 2 37-mm AA; 6 MGs (twins)
A/S weapons	Depth charge projectors (some have 2 5-barrelled MBUs)
Main engines	3 diesels; 3 shafts; 3,300 hp
Speed, knots	24
Range, miles	1,500 at 12 knots
Complement	65

Built in 1948–56. Flush-decked with large squat funnel, slightly raked, and massive block bridge structure. Now being phased out of service due to age. About twenty ships were rebuilt as communications relay ships of the "Libau" class.

Radar. *Pot Head.*

Soviet Type Name. *Maly Protivo Lodochny Korabl,* meaning Small Anti-Submarine Ship.

Transfers. Bulgaria (2), China (24), Cuba (18), Indonesia (14), Poland (8), Romania (3).

5 "T 43"/AGR Class

Displacement, tons	500 standard; 610 full load
Dimensions, feet (*metres*)	190·2 × 28·2 × 6·9 (*58·0 × 8·6 × 2·1*)
Guns	4 37-mm AA; 2 25-mm AA
Main engines	2 diesels; 2 shafts; 2,000 bhp
Speed, knots	17
Range, miles	1,600 at 10 knots
Complement	60

Former fleet minesweepers of the "T.43" class converted into radar pickets with comprehensive electronic equipment. It is reported that there may be a dozen vessels of this type. A large *Big Net*-like radar is mounted on the mainmast.

"T.43"/AGR class
(*S. Breyer*)

Light Forces

The successful operations of the 55-foot CMBs of the Royal Navy against the Soviet Fleet in Kronstadt Roads on 18 August 1919 might well have suggested to the new regime that here lay a cheap but effective means of supplementing their largely moribund navy. Twenty-four coastal patrol craft of First World War US-construction were listed in 1924, 60-foot boats with a speed of 25 knots. Whether these really did survive at this date it is impossible to say but what is certain is that in May 1927 John I. Thornycroft & Co. Ltd. delivered two 55-foot CMBs to the USSR, craft in most particulars identical to those used in Kronstadt eight years earlier. These carried two 18-inch torpedoes in stern troughs, a method of launching adhered to in all the craft of pre-war design. A large number of these were of the Italian MAS design which were being built in considerable numbers in Italy in the mid-1930s. Both craft and engines were built under licence in the USSR, varying from 6 to 35 tons with speeds ranging up to 45 knots. The most numerous class was the "G5" which first appeared in 1935. A 17-ton, 45-knot design this, with the 35-ton "D-3" class, was kept in production throughout the war. The numbers in Light Forces, which started the war with some 140 craft, was also kept up by the transfer of about 200 torpedo-boats of various designs by the USA.

After 1945 various indigenous designs were put in hand, the first being the "PA1" class (later "P2") which carried two 18-inch torpedoes and two machine-guns. These were launched between 1946–50 and were immediately followed in 1951 by the "PA2" class (later "P4") which continued in production until 1958. This 22-ton, 63-foot class has an aluminium alloy hull and diesel engines and they were the first Soviet boats to mount torpedo-tubes – in this case 18-inch. Their successors, the "PA3" class (later "P6"), were of a totally different design, bearing a considerable similarity to some of the ex-US craft which were held on the Soviet list until 1963. When the first of what was ultimately to be some 600 "P6s" appeared in 1953–4 she was seen to have a length/beam ratio of 4 : 1 as against the $5\frac{1}{2}$: 1 of the "P4s". Wooden hulled and more stable than the "P4s" this class was of 66 tons and their four diesels produced 43 knots.

Their torpedo armament had been increased to two 21-inch tubes and two twin 25-mm mounts in place of the "P4"s Machine guns. Various modifications to the basic "P6" design appeared from time to time. The first was probably the "P8/10" variant which was notable for being the first Soviet attempt at using the maritime gas-turbine. As well as this innovation the "P8" was provided with hydrofoils forward to increase stability. It seems unlikely that this lash-up achieved much success and the fact that the funnels on the gas-turbine boats have become much rarer suggests that this form of propulsion, too, was not a particular success. The third variation on the "P6" theme was the "MO VI" in which the torpedo-tubes were discarded in place of extra depth-charges and two throwers. Some seventy to eighty of these appeared in the last four years of the 1950s.

Between 1960–62 the fourth "P6" conversion entered service, the "Komar". This must have posed many problems of stability for the designers because, with the after 25-mm mount and both torpedo-tubes removed, two SSN-2 (*Styx*) missile launchers were fitted, (one either side of the bridge) and a new search radar was fitted on a lattice-mast. The *Styx* missiles themselves weigh probably twice as much as a torpedo and the ancillary fittings probably account for a good deal more. Whatever the problems, up to 100 of this class were completed with many more being sent to client countries.

Adding to this new dimension in naval warfare, the first occasion on which guided missiles in fast attack craft has been added to the already complex problems of naval tactics, was the entirely newly designed "Osa" class. On a 200-ton hull these craft mounted four SSN-2 missiles and were capable of 32–35 knots. The hull, for the first time in Soviet fast attack craft, was made of steel and the armament was increased by the mounting of two twin 30-mm gun mountings, "Osa I" appeared in 1960–61 – in the mid-1960s came "Osa II" in which the *Styx* launch tubes were considerably modified. They were now totally enclosed, smaller and lighter, advantages which were probably achieved by the use of a modified *Styx* missile (SSN-11) in which the wings folded.

In the same way as the "P6" hull was used for other variants so the "Osa" hull was used in the construction of the thirty-five "Stenka" class. With the missile launchers removed four 16-inch A/S torpedo-tubes were fitted and depth-charge racks shipped. The forward profile has been altered from that of the "Osas" by the building up of the bridge and the fitting of solid bulwarks. The first of the "Stenkas" appeared in 1967 – four years before that the "Shershen" fast attack craft (torpedo) had been produced. The hull form of this class appears similar to that of the "Osas" but some 15 feet shorter at 115 feet. With the same engines as "Osa" she is capable of over 40 knots and carries, in addition to the same two twin 30-mm, four 21-inch tubes, two depth-charge racks for twelve charges and a pair of mine rails.

In 1964 the first naval application of the hydrofoil appeared, the

"Pchela" class. These were small 80-ton craft, a simple conversion of the "Strela" class ferry. With a good radar fit and two twin machine-gun mounts these are clearly high-speed patrol craft, all twenty-five now being operated by the KGB. Their successors, the "Turya" class, began to enter service in 1973. Much larger craft at 165 tons these mount four 21-inch tubes, a twin 57-mm aft and a pair of 25-mm forward. On the transom a form of VDS is fitted, although there is no sign of normal A/S weapons.

The USSR today has an inventory of Light Forces surpassed only by the Chinese and, backed by considerable River Patrol Forces and with hovercraft development in full swing, this provides a very considerable coastal defence force as well as giving unrivalled opportunities for the training of young officers.

LIGHT FORCES

120 "Osa I and II" Class (65 I and 55 II)
(Fast Attack Craft – Missile)

Displacement, tons	165 standard; 200 full load
Dimensions, feet (*metres*)	128·7 × 25·1 × 5·9 (*39·3 × 7·7 × 1·8*)
Missile launchers	4 in two pairs abreast for SSN-2A or SSN-11
Guns	4 30-mm; (2 twin, 1 forward, 1 aft)
Main engines	3 diesels; 13,000 bhp
Speed, knots	32 knots
Range, miles	800 at 25 knots
Complement	30

"Osa I" (right) and
"Osa II" class *(Tass)*

These boats, built since 1960, have a larger hull and four launchers in two pairs as compared with one pair in the "Komar" class. They have a surface-to-surface missile range of up to 23 miles. Later boats have cylindrical missile launchers, comprising the "Osa II" class which appeared in the mid-1960s.

This class was a revolution in naval shipbuilding. Although confined by their size and range to coastal operations the lethality and accuracy of the *Styx* missile have already been proved by the sinking of the Israeli destroyer *Eilat* on 21 October 1967 by an Egyptian "Komar". The operations of the Indian "Osas" in the war with Pakistan in December 1971 were equally successful against merchant vessels by night. These operations surely represent a most important lesson in naval operations and, in light of this, the list of transfers should be noted.

Radar. *Square Tie* and *Drum Tilt*.

Transfers. Algeria (3), Bulgaria (3), China (17), Cuba (5), Egypt (12), East Germany (12), India (8), Iraq (6), North Korea (8), Poland (12), Romania (5), Syria (6), Yugoslavia (10).

15 "Komar" Class
(Fast Attack Craft – Missile)

"Komar" class

Displacement, tons	70 standard; 80 full load
Dimensions, feet (*metres*)	83·7 × 19·8 × 5·0 (*25·5 × 6·0 × 1·5*)
Missile launchers	2 for SSN-2A system
Guns	2 25-mm AA (1 twin forward)
Range, miles	400 at 30 knots
Main engines	4 diesels; 4 shafts; 4,800 bhp
Speed, knots	40
Complement	20

A smaller type of boat converted from "P 6" class torpedo boats. Fitted with two surface-to-surface launchers aft in a hooded casing approximately 45 degrees to the deck line with a range of 23 miles. First units completed 1961. Being phased out of service.

Radar. *Square Tie.*

Transfers. Algeria (6), China (10), Cuba (18), Egypt (6), Indonesia (12), North Korea (10), Syria (3).

45 "Stenka" Class
(Fast Attack Craft – Patrol)

"Stenka" class

Displacement, tons	170 standard; 210 full load
Dimensions, feet (*metres*)	128·7 × 25·1 × 5·9 (*39·3 × 7·7 × 1·8*)
Guns	4 30-mm AA (2 twin)
Torpedo tubes	4 16-in (*406-mm*) anti-submarine
A/S weapons	2 depth charge racks
Main engines	3 diesels; 10,000 bhp
Speed, knots	40
Complement	25

Based on the hull design of the "Osa" class. Built from 1967–68 onwards.

Radar. Search: *Square Tie*. Fire Control: *Drum Tilt, Pot Drum*.

12 "Turya" Class
(Fast Attack Craft – Patrol Hydrofoil)

Displacement, tons	165
Dimensions, feet (*metres*)	123 × 27·9 × 5·9 (*37·5 × 8·5 × 1·8*)
Guns	2 57-mm (twin, aft); 2 25-mm (twin, fwd)
Torpedo tubes	4 21-inch
Speed, knots	40

"Turya" class
(*S. Breyer*)

A new class of hydrofoils with a naval orientation rather than the earlier "Pchela" class. Entered service from 1973 – in series production, prossibly three per year.

Radar. *Pot Drum* and *Drum Tilt*.

Sonar. A form of VDS is fitted on the transom. In view of this the apparent lack of A/S weapons is surprising. Could operate with shore-based helicopters.

25 "Pchela" Class
(Fast Attack Craft – Torpedo Hydrofoil)

"Pchela" class

Displacement, tons	70 standard; 80 full load
Dimensions, feet (*metres*)	82·0 × 19·7 (*25·0 × 6·0*)
Guns	4 MG (2 twin)
Main engines	2 diesels; 6,000 bhp
Speed, knots	50

This class of hydrofoils, is reported to have been built since 1964–65. Also carry depth charges. Used for frontier guard duties by KGB.

45 "Shershen" Class
(Fast Attack Craft – Torpedo)

Displacement, tons	150 standard; 160 full load
Dimensions, feet (*metres*)	115·5 × 23·1 × 5·0 (*35·2 × 7·0 × 1·5*)
Guns	4 30-mm AA (2 twin)
Tubes	4 21-in (single)
A/S weapons	12 DC
Main engines	Diesels; 3 shafts; 13,000 bhp
Speed, knots	41
Complement	16

Radar. *Pot Drum* and *Drum Tilt*. IFF: *High Pole*.

Transfers. Bulgaria (4), East Germany (15), Egypt (6), Yugoslavia (13).

"Shershen" class
(*S. Breyer*)

80 "P 6" "P 8" "P 10" Classes
(Fast Attack Craft – Torpedo)

Displacement, tons	66 standard: 75 full load
Dimensions, feet (*metres*)	84·2 × 20·0 × 6·0 (*25·7 × 6·1 × 1·8*)
Guns	4 25-mm AA
Tubes	2 21-in (or mines, or depth charges)
Main engines	4 diesels; 4 shafts; 4,800 bhp; Gas-turbines in "P 8" and "P 10" classes
Speed, knots	43
Range, miles	450 at 30 knots
Complement	25

Top: "P6" class;
centre: "P8" class;
bottom: "P10" class
(S. Breyer)

The "P 6" class was of a standard medium–sized type running into series production. Launched during 1957 to 1960. Known as "MO VI" class in the FAC (patrol) version. The later versions, known as the "P 8" and "P 10" classes, were powered with gas-turbines, having different bridge and funnel, "P 8" boats have hydrofoils. This class is now being deleted because of old age.

Transfers. Algeria (12), China (80, indigenous construction), Cuba (12), Egypt (24), East Germany (18), Guinea (4), Indonesia (14), Iraq (12), Nigeria (3), Poland (20), North Vietnam (6), Somalia (2).

15 "MO VI" Class
(Fast Attack Craft – Patrol)

Displacement, tons	64 standard; 73 full load
Dimensions, feet (*metres*)	84·2 × 20 × 4·0 (*25·7 × 6·1 × 1·2*)
Guns	4 25-mm AA (2 twin)
A/S weapons	2 depth charge mortars; 2 depth charge racks
Main engines	4 diesels; 4 shafts; 4,800 bhp
Speed, knots	40

Built in 1956 to 1960. Based on the hull design of the "P 6".

10 "P 4" Class
(Fast Attack Craft – Torpedo)

Displacement, tons	22
Dimensions, feet (*metres*)	62·7 × 11·6 × 5·6 (*19·1 × 3·5 × 1·7*)
Guns	2 15-mm MG (twin)
Tubes	2 18-in
Main engines	2 diesels; 2 shafts; 2,200 bhp
Speed, knots	50
Complement	12

Originally a numerically large class of boats with aluminium alloy hulls. Launched in 1951–58. The earlier units are being discarded.

Transfers. Albania (12), Bulgaria (8), China (70), Cuba (12), Cyprus (6), North Korea (40), Romania (13), Somalia (4), Syria (17).

RIVER PATROL CRAFT
Attached to Black Sea and Pacific Fleets for operations on the Danube, Amur and Usuri Rivers, and to the Caspian Flotilla.

40 "Schmel" Class

Displacement, tons	120
Length, feet (*metres*)	92 (*28·1*)
Guns	1 76-mm; 2 25-mm (twin)
Speed, knots	20
Complement	15

Forward gun mounted in a tank-type turret. Some also mount a 10-barrelled rocket launcher amidships. Built between 1958 and 1966.

"Schmel" class
(*J. Rowe*)

"Schmel" class (*Tass*)

30 "BK 3" Class

Displacement, tons	120
Length, feet (*metres*)	95 (*29·0*)
Guns	1 76-mm; 4 MG (twin mounts)
Speed, knots	22
Complement	20

Not unlike the "Schmel" class but with an additional MG mounting at after-end of the waist.

20 "BKL 4" Class

Displacement, tons	60
Length, feet (*metres*)	55 (*16·8*)
Guns	2 20-mm; 6 MG
Speed, knots	28

PS 10

Displacement, tons	approx 250
Guns	2 20-mm
Speed, knots	15

Acts as Senior Officer's ship for the Danube squadron.

Top right: "Rok 9" class. Above: "Bk 3" class. Right: "PS-10" class (*Jurg Meister*)

"PR" Class

Displacement, tons   90
Dimensions, feet (*metres*) 88 × 18 × 3 (*26·8 × 5·5 × 1·0*)
Guns   1 76-mm; 2 25-mm
Speed, knots   25

ROK 9

Of approximately 100 tons – probably acts as support ship to Danube squadron.

Mine Warfare Forces

The static mine, in its earliest moored form and its later ground variety, has been a matter of the greatest interest in Russian naval circles for more than a century. Brought face-to-face with its menace during the Russo-Japanese War of 1904–05, they used it with considerable effect in the Gulf of Riga during the First World War. In the earliest days of the Soviet Navy not only were there numerous specialised minelayers capable of carrying 300–600 mines each but all the available light cruisers, destroyers and submarines were fitted for this purpose. This capability was continued in subsequent designs up to and including the "Sverdlovs" (150 mines) and the "Kotlins" and "Skorys" (80 mines each). In subsequent classes this facet of operations has been disregarded although some reports suggest that the "Kashins" and "Krivaks" may be so fitted. If so this would be an unusual reversal of policy which, with the removal of a mining capability, had taken away the element of "home defence" in favour of longer range requirements.

There is little doubt that the USSR with its "mine consciousness" built up large stocks of this weapon in the immediate post-war years as part of the defensive policy then in vogue. That these most likely now include not only moored mines but advanced versions of magnetic, acoustic and pressure mines there is little doubt. Quantities have been supplied to various client states and their use at such widely separated points in space and time as Korea in 1951–53 and Egypt's Red Sea approaches in 1973 show that this is a menace which should prompt some apprehension. The seventy or so surface ships of the USSR capable of mine-laying would certainly be joined by the two specialised "Alesha" class, a large force of submarines undoubtedly having a mine-laying capability in lieu of re-load torpedoes and, possibly, aircraft fitted for the same task.

While certain Western navies have allowed their mine-sweeping forces and minehunters to run down at a time of financial stringency and have investigated, and operated, alternatives such as helicopters and hovercraft the Soviet Navy has continued a steady building programme throughout the post-war years. In 1940 only some 20–30 minesweepers were listed, the majority being conversions of fairly elderly vessels such as tugs. By the mid-1950s this total had increased to about 150 mine-sweepers (Ocean) and 220 minesweepers (Coastal). In each case less than half were Soviet designed and built, the remainder being either lease-lend, or taken over at the war's end. The Ocean sweepers of Russian parentage were the forty "Fuga" (or "Tral") class, 540-ton ships of an early 1930s design, and the thirty or so 800-ton "Vasili Gromov" class which were all soon to be on the disposal list.

Between 1948–57 the customary Soviet mass-production of a chosen class resulted in the building of 175 ships of the "T43" class of Ocean sweepers. Of 610 tons with a cruising range of 1,600 miles and a top speed of 17 knots these have become well-known abroad in the navies of the friends of the USSR, as well as in other forms such as radar pickets. As their production ceased so the new "T58" class appeared and from 1957 to 1964 about forty were built. Of 900-tons and 18-knots fourteen were converted to submarine rescue ships ("Valday" class) and one became an "AG1" (*Gidrolog*). Their successors of the "Yurka" class, which entered service in 1963 and of which forty-five were built in the ensuing five years, were smaller at 550 tons. These were steel-hulled ships as were those of the follow-on "Natya" class which first appeared in 1971 and is still (1975) in series production at the rate of about three a year.

The coastal sweepers of the mid-1950s, apart from British, Dutch, German and US craft, included a number of the "T301" class, the first of which had been commissioned in 1946–47. Of 180 tons and 17 knots about 230 were built before production ceased in 1956 to be followed by the larger (280-ton) "Sasha" class. These steel-hulled ships were not long in production, totalling only fifty and being followed in 1961 by the first of the "Vanya" class of about the same size but with a wooden hull. Seventy of these were built before the appearance of the "Zhenya" class in 1972. Only about three of these were built and it has been reported that they were a trial class with GRP hulls. If this is so their immediate success-ors of the "Sonya" class (1973) are probably the production GRP model of about 320 tons and fitted with both mine and influence sweeping. So far there is no evidence of a specific class of minehunters being designed although, with Soviet advances in sonar design, this must be on the cards.

Including some 100 elderly inshore minesweepers of the "TR40" (60 tons) and "K8" (70 tons) classes the total of the Soviet minesweeping force is today (1975) just over 400, of which over half must be considered out-of-date. Nevertheless it does provide an adequate number for such tasks as port-approach clearance, sweeping-in an amphibious force or the provision of swept channels in straits and other mineable waters. In view of Soviet interest in helicopters and hovercraft it would be no surprise to see these aircraft becoming a support force for the ships.

MINE WARFARE FORCES

Note: The "Alesha" class (under Support and Depot Ships) probably has a primary minelaying role.

16 "Natya" Class
(Minesweepers – Ocean)

Displacement, tons	650 full load
Dimensions, feet (*metres*)	200·1 × 34·1 × 7·2 (*61·0 × 10·4 × 2·2*)
Guns	4 30-mm AA (2 twin); 4 25-mm AA (2 twin)
A/S weapons	2 5-barrelled MBUs
Main engines	2 diesels; 5,000 bhp
Speed, knots	18

A new class of fleet minesweepers first reported in 1971, evidently intended as successors to the "Yurka" class. Building rate of three a year.

"Natya" class

45 "Yurka" Class
(Minesweepers – Ocean)

Displacement, tons	450 full load
Dimensions, feet (*metres*)	171·9 × 31 × 8·9 (*52·4 × 9·5 × 2·7*)
Guns	4 30-mm AA (2 twin)
Main engines	2 diesels; 4,000 bhp
Speed, knots	18

A class of medium fleet minesweepers with steel hull. Built from 1963 to the late 1960s.

"Yurka" class

Transfer. 4 to Egypt.

20 "T 58" Class
(Minesweepers – Ocean)

Displacement, tons	790 standard; 900 full load
Dimensions, feet (*metres*)	229·9 × 29·5 × 7·9 (*70·1 × 9·0 × 2·4*)
A/S weapons	2 5-barrelled MBUs
Guns	4 57-mm AA (2 twin)
Main engines	2 diesels; 2 shafts; 4,000 bhp
Speed, knots	18

Built from 1957 to 1964. Of this class fourteen were converted to submarine rescue ships with armament and sweeping gear removed, see later page ("Valdai" class).

110 "T 43" Class
(Minesweepers – Ocean)

Displacement, tons	500 standard; 610 full load
Dimensions, feet (*metres*)	190·2 × 28·2 × 6·9 (*58·0 × 8·6 × 2·1*)
Guns	4 37-mm AA (2 twin); 4 25-mm AA (2 twin)
Main engines	2 diesels; 2 shafts; 2,000 bhp
Speed, knots	17
Range, miles	1,600 at 10 knots
Complement	40

Built in 1948–57 in shipyards throughout the Soviet Union. A number of this class were converted into radar pickets. The remainder are gradually being replaced by newer types of fleet minesweepers.

Transfers. Algeria (2), Albania (2), Bulgaria (2), China (20), Egypt (6), Indonesia (6), Poland (12), Syria (2).

"T 58" class

"T 43" class

3 "Sonya" Class

Displacement, tons	400
Length, feet (*metres*)	154·1 (*47*)

A new design of MSC first reported in 1973. Now in series production. Probably uses a GRP hull.

3 "Zhenya" Class
(Minesweepers – Coastal)

Displacement, tons	320
Dimensions, feet (*metres*)	141 × 25 × 7 (*43·0 × 7·6 × 2·1*)
Guns	2 30-mm (twin)
Main engines	2 diesels
Speed, knots	18

Reported to be a trial class for GRP hulls. First reported in 1972.

"Zhenya" class

70 "Vanya" Class
(Minesweepers – Coastal)

Displacement, tons	225 standard; 250 full load
Dimensions, feet (*metres*)	130·7 × 24 × 6·9 (*39·9 × 7·3 × 2·1*)
Guns	2 30-mm AA (1 twin)
Main engines	2 diesels; 2,200 bhp
Speed, knots	18
Complement	30

A coastal class with wooden hulls of a type suitable for series production built from 1961 onwards. Basically similar to NATO-type coastal minesweepers.

"Vanya" class

40 "Sasha" Class
(Minesweepers – Coastal)

Displacement, tons	245 standard; 280 full load
Dimensions, feet (*metres*)	150·9 × 20·5 × 6·6 (*46·0 × 6·3 × 2·0*)
Guns	1 57-mm dp; 4 25-mm AA (2 twin)
Main engines	2 diesels; 2,200 bhp
Speed, knots	18
Complement	25

Basically similar to NATO coastal minesweepers, but of steel construction. About fifty built between 1956–1960.

5 "T 301" Class
(Minesweepers – Coastal)

Displacement, tons   150 standard; 180 full load
Dimensions, feet (*metres*) 128·0 × 18·0 × 4·9 (*39·0 × 5·5 × 1·5*)
Guns   2 37-mm AA; 4 MG (twin)
Main engines   2 diesels; 2 shafts; 1,440 bhp
Speed, knots   17

Built from 1946 to 1956. Several were converted to survey craft, and many adapted for other purposes or used for port duty and auxiliary service. Now being withdrawn form service due to age.

"TR 40" Class
(Minesweepers – Inshore)

Displacement, tons   40 standard; 60 full load
Dimensions, feet (*metres*) 55·8 × 11·5 × 4·0 (*17·0 × 3·5 × 1·2*)
Guns   2 25-mm (twin) 2 MG (twin)
Main engines   Diesels
Speed, knots   18

"K 8" Class
(Minesweepers – Inshore)

Displacement, tons   50 standard; 70 full load
Dimensions, feet (*metres*) 92·0 × 13·5 × 2·3 (*28·0 × 4·1 × 0·7*)
Guns   2 MG (twin)
Main engines   Diesels; 600 bhp
Speed, knots   14

Auxiliary motor minesweeping boats of the inshore ("TR 40") and river ("K 8") types. A total of about 100 of both classes in service.

Amphibious Forces

There is little that need be added here to the comments already given in the main body of the text. In the mid 1950s the total of Soviet amphibious forces was a mixture of two ex-Japanese and one ex-Italian transports and about 100 landing-craft. The majority of these were ex-Germans of 150 or 230 tons with forty-seven ex-US LSILs and LCUs and a small number of ex-Italian MZ craft.

The fact that the earliest of the Soviet-designed landing craft of the "MP 2", "4", "6" and "8" classes were built in the late 1950s suggests that Admiral Gorshkov himself, after his accession to power in January 1956, may have had a considerable influence on their production. The "MP 10" and "Vydra" classes followed in the 1960s, while the "Polnocny" class LCTs began to appear in 1963 and the 5,800-ton "Alligator" class LSTs were first delivered in 1965–66. Both these classes were built in a number of variations but have basically remained the core of the Soviet amphibious forces. A new class of LCTs, the "Ropucha", was first reported in 1974 and, like so many of the "Polnocnys", is under construction in Poland for the USSR.

Some people are inclined to belittle the size of the LST/LCT force, only twelve and sixty respectively. They would do well to remember the vast number of ships in the Soviet merchant marine and the fact that these, as Government run vessels, can be switched to naval operations with a minimum of delay.

AMPHIBIOUS FORCES

12 "Alligator" Class (LST)

Displacement, tons	4,100 standard; 5,800 full load
Dimensions, feet (*metres*)	370·7 × 50·9 × 12·1 (*113·0 × 15·5 × 3·7*)
Guns	2 57-mm AA
Main engines	Diesels; 8,000 bhp
Speed, knots	15

Aleksandr Tortsev
Donetsky Shakhter
Krasnaya Presnya
Krymsky Komsomolets
Petr Ilichev
Tomsky Komsomolets
Voronezhsky Komsomolets
+5

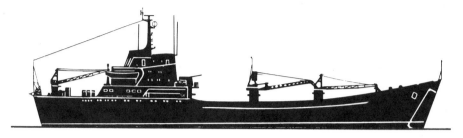

Largest type of landing ship built in the USSR to date. First ship built in 1965–66 and commissioned in 1966. These ships have ramps on the bow and stern. Carrying capacity 1,700 tons. There are three variations of rig. In earlier type two or three cranes are carried – later types have only one crane. In the third type the bridge structure has been raised and the forward deckhouse has been considerably lengthened.

60 "Polnocny" Class (LCT)

(Note – A new class of LCTs, the "Ropucha" class, of which details are not available, has been reported as building in Poland).

Displacement, tons	700 standard; 800 full load (Type IX 1,300)
Dimensions, feet (*metres*)	239·4 × 29·5 × 9·8 (*73·0 × 9·0 × 3·0*)
	(Type IX 285 × 27·7 × 9·8) (*86·9 × 8·4 × 3·0*)
Guns	2 30-mm (twin) in all but earliest ships (see note)
A/S weapons	2 18-barrelled MBU
Main engines	2 diesels; 5,000 bhp
Speed, knots	18

"Alligator" class
LST *Krymsky
Komsomolets*

Carrying capacity 350 tons. Can carry six tanks. Up to nine types of this class have been built. In I to IV the mast and funnel are combined; in V onwards the mast is stepped on the bridge; in VI to VIII there is a redesign of the bow-form; IX is a completely new design of greater length with corresponding increase in tonnage and with four 30-mm (two twins).

"Polnocny IX" class LCT (*S. Breyer*)

Radar. *Muff Cob.*

Transfers. 3 to Egypt, 3 to India, 2 to S. Yemen.

35 "Vydra" Class (LCU)

Displacement, tons   300 standard; 500 full load
Dimensions, feet (*metres*) 157·4 × 24·6 × 7·2 (*48·0 × 7·5 × 2·2*)
Main engines   2 diesels; 2 shafts; 400 hp
Speed, knots   15

A new class of landing craft of the LCU type. Built from 1967–69. No armament. Carrying capacity 250 tons.

Transfers. 10 to Egypt.

8 "MP 2" Class (LCU)

Displacement, tons   750
Dimensions, feet (*metres*) 190 × 25 × 8·2 (*58·0 × 7·6 × 2·5*)
Guns   6 25-mm (twins)
Main engines   Diesels; 1,200 hp
Speed, knots   16

Built 1956–60. Carrying capacity 200 tons.

"MP 4" class *(J. Rowe)*

15 "MP 4" Class (LCU)

Displacement, tons   800 full load
Dimensions, feet *(metres)* 183·7 × 26·2 × 8·9 *(56·0 × 8·0 × 2·7)*
Guns   4 25-mm (2 twin)
Main engines   Diesels; 2 shafts; 1,100 bhp
Speed, knots   12

Built in 1956–58. Of the small freighter type in appearance. Two masts, one abaft the bridge and one in the waist. Gun mountings on poop and forecastle. Can carry 6 to 8 tanks. Several ships now serve as transports.

8 "MP 6" Class (LCU)

Displacement, tons   2,000
Dimensions, feet *(metres)* 246 × 40 × 10·5 *(75·0 × 12·2 × 3·2)*
Guns   4 45-mm (quad)
Main engines   Diesels; 2,400 hp
Speed, knots   14

Ex-merchant ship hulls. Carrying capacity 500 tons. Built 1958–61.

5 "MP 8" Class (LCU)

Displacement, tons   800 standard; 1,200 full load
Dimensions, feet *(metres)* 239·5 × 34·8 × 15·1 *(73·0 × 10·6 × 4·6)*
Guns   4 57-mm (2 twin)
Main engines   Diesels; 4,000 bhp
Speed, knots   15

Have a short and low quarter deck abaft the funnel. Can carry 6 tanks. Carrying capacity 400 tons. Built 1958–61.

Left: "MP 8" class
(*S. Breyer*)
below: "MP 10" class

10 "MP 10" Class (LCU)

Displacement, tons   200 standard; 420 full load
Dimensions, feet (*metres*) 157·5 × 21·3 × 6·5 (*48·0 × 6·5 × 2·0*)
Main engines   2 diesels; 2 shafts; 400 hp
Speed, knots   11

A type of landing craft basically similar to the British LCT (4) type in silhouette and layout. Can carry 4 tanks. Loading capacity about 150 tons. Built 1959–66.

"T 4" Class (LCM)

Main engines   3 diesels; 3 shafts; 3,300 bhp
Speed, knots   24
Range, miles   1,500 at 12 knots

Hydrofoil Type

A small landing craft of 92 feet length capable of carrying 2–3 tanks.

AIR CUSHION VEHICLES

(Numbers in service are not known. The following gives an indication of Soviet capability. Fuller details appear in *Jane's Surface Skimmers 1974-75*).

Research Hovercraft

Operating weight, tons   15
Dimensions, feet (*metres*) 70 × 30 (*21·4 × 9·2*)
Propulsion   2 350-hp aircraft radial engines
Lift   1 350-hp aircraft radial with centrifugal fan
Speed, knots   50

159

Right: Research
Hovercraft; Centre:
"Skate" class; Below:
Ekranoplan *(Jane's
Surface Skimmers)*

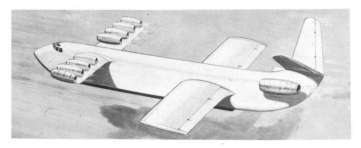

In use in the Soviet Navy since 1967 for tests and evaluation.

"Skate" Class

Operating weight, tons 27
Dimensions, feet *(metres)* 67·5 × 24 *(20·6 × 7·3)*
Propulsion 2 780-hp marine gas turbines (VP and reversible
    propellers)
Lift 1 780-hp marine gas turbine
Speed, knots 58
Range, miles 230 cruising

This is a naval version of a fifty-seat passenger carrying craft, probably in use
for the Naval Infantry.

160

Assault Craft

Operating weight, tons   200 approx
Dimensions, feet (*metres*) 130 × 80 approx (*39·7 × 24·4*)
Speed, knots   70 approx

Currently undergoing trials for Naval Infantry. Is the first large Soviet amphibious hovercraft. Similar to British SR.N4.

Ekranoplan Craft (WIG)

Dimensions, feet (*metres*) 400 × 125 (*122·0 × 38·1*) (approx wing span)
Propulsion   10 gas turbines (two to assist take-off then eight
                           for cruising)
Speed, knots   300 approx

An experimental craft, a wing-in-ground-effect machine, with a carrying capacity of about 900 troops and with potential for a number of naval applications such as ASW, minesweeping or patrol. Claimed to be capable of operations in heavy weather as well as crossing marshes, ice and low obstacles.

Support and Depot Ships

The Soviet Navy in the mid 1950s was supplied with fifteen ships in this group, a somewhat motley collection of converted merchant ships and ex-German vessels. Conversions continued with the "Tovda" repair ships (1958) and the "Atrek" submarine-support ships (1956–58). At the same time a custom built class, the "Dneprs", appeared, apparently designed for repair work on submarines and in 1957 the first of the "Don" class entered service. At 9,500 tons she was the largest such ship in the Soviet service and six of the class were completed by 1962. In this year the "Ugra" class, an improved "Don", began to join the fleet. Of the same tonnage as the "Dons" the most obvious improvement was the provision of proper helicopter facilities and a hangar. The "Ugra"'s armament was less than that of the earlier "Dons", the latter having four 100-mm guns in addition to eight 57-mm. In the "Ugras", as in the later "Dons", the 100-mm guns were left out. These sixteen ships, all capable of 20 knots and with a range of 10,000 miles at 12 knots, provide the main bulk of the Soviet submarine support effort abroad. Supported by the smaller general purpose repair ships of the "Oskol" (ten units) and "Amur" (twelve units) classes a very considerable repair and maintenance capability has been provided.

More specialised are the five ships of the 7,000-ton "Lama" class and the single "Amga". All these are reported as having a missile support facility and the fact that the "Amga" appeared in 1974 and is supplied with a much larger crane than the "Lamas" (which were built from 1960 onwards) suggests that her purpose is to handle the submarine-launched SSN-8 and possibly SSNX-13 missiles.

With these support and depot ships working in collaboration with the increasing numbers of fleet support ships such as *Boris Chilikin*, the Soviet Navy has been provided with a considerable capability during long foreign deployments which it has never had before.

SUPPORT AND DEPOT SHIPS

(Submarine depot ship)
Borodino
Gangut
Ivan Kolyshkin
Ivan Kucherenko
Tobol
Volga
+4

10 "Ugra" Class
(Submarine Depot Ship)

Displacement, tons	6,750 standard; 7,000 full load
Length, feet (*metres*)	463·8 (*141·4*)
Beam, feet (*metres*)	57·6 (*17·6*)
Aircraft	1 helicopter
Guns	8 57-mm (twin)
Range, miles	10,000 at 12 knots

Improved versions of the "Don" class. Built from 1961 onwards, all in Niko-layev. Equipped with workshops. Provided with a helicopter platform and, in later versions, a hangar. Carries a large derrick to handle torpedoes. Has mooring points in hull about 100 feet apart, and has baggage ports possibly for coastal craft and submarines. The last pair of this class mount a large super-structure from the mainmast to quarter-deck, and are used for training.

Radar. *Strut Curve. Muff Cob. Don.*

Transfer. *Amba*, of this class, which had 4 76-mm guns, was transferred to India.

"Ugra" class

6 "Don" Class
(Submarine Support)

Dmitri Galkin
Fedor Vidyaev
Magomed Gadzhiev
Mikhail Tukaevsky
Nikolay Stolbov
Viktor Kotelnikov

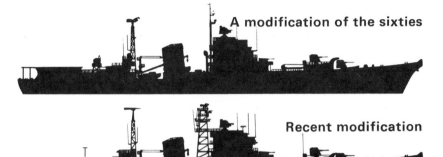

Original version

A modification of the sixties

Recent modification

"Don" class *Dimitri Galkin*

Displacement, tons	6,700 standard; 7,000 full load
Length, feet (*metres*)	458·9 (*139·9*)
Beam, feet (*metres*)	57·7 (*17·6*)
Draught, feet (*metres*)	22·3 (*6·8*)
Aircraft	Provision for helicopter in two ships
Guns	4 3·9 (*100-mm*); 8 57-mm (4 twin) (see *notes*)
Main engines	4 or 6 diesels; 14,000 bhp
Speed, knots	21
Complement	300

Support ships, all named after officers lost in WW II. Built in 1957 to 1962. Originally seven ships were built all in Nikolayev. Quarters for about 350 submariners.

Gunnery. In hull number III only 2 3·9-in. In IV no 3·9-in mounted. In some of class 8 25-mm (twin) are mounted.

Radar. Search: *Slim Net* and probably *Strut Curve*. Fire Control: *Hawk Screech* (2).

Transfers. 1 to Indonesia in 1962.

1 "Purga" Class

Displacement, tons	2,250 standard; 3,000 full load
Length, feet (*metres*)	324·8 (*99·0*)
Beam, feet (*metres*)	44·3 (*13·5*)
Draught, feet (*metres*)	17·1 (*5·2*)
Guns	4 3·9-in (*100-mm*) singles; 2 25-mm
Mines	50 capacity
Main engines	Diesels
Speed, knots	18
Complement	250

Laid down in 1939 in Leningrad and completed in 1948. Sturdy ocean-going general-purpose ship equipped as icebreaker, escort, training ship and tender. Fitted with directors similar to those in the "Riga" class frigates. Modernised in 1958–60.

"Purga" class

5 "Lama" Class
(Missile Support)

Displacement, tons	4,600 full load
Length, feet (*metres*)	370·0 (*112·8*) oa
Beam, feet (*metres*)	47·2 (*14·4*)
Draught, feet (*metres*)	19·0 (*5·8*)
Guns	8 57-mm, 2 quadruple, 1 on the forecastle; 1 on the break of the quarter-deck
Main engines	Diesels; 2 shafts; 5,000 shp
Speed, knots	15

The engines are sited aft to allow for a very large and high hangar or hold amidships for carrying missiles or weapons spares. This is about 12 feet high above the main deck. There are doors at the forward end with rails leading in and a raised turntable gantry or travelling cranes for transferring armaments to combatant ships.

There are mooring points along the hull for ships of low freeboard such as submarines to come alongside. The well deck is about 40 feet long, enough for a missile to fit horizontally before being lifted vertically for loading.

Radar. Search: *Slim Net* and *Strut Curve*. Fire Control: *Hawk Screech* (2).

"Lama" class
(*Skyfotos*)

1 "Amga" Class
(Missile Support)

Displacement, tons	approx 5,500
Dimensions, feet *(metres)*	361 × 56 × 19 (*110 × 17 × 5·8*)
Guns	4 30-mm (twins)
Main engines	Diesels
Speed, knots	18

A single ship of similar size and duties to the "Lama" class. May be distinguished from those ships by the break at the bridge, giving a lower freeboard than that of the "Lamas". She is fitted with a large crane forward and is thus capable of handling much larger missiles than her predecessors. Probably, therefore, designed for servicing submarines, particularly those armed with SSN-8 missiles.

075
083

2 "Alesha" Class
(Minelayers)

Displacement, tons	3,600 standard; 4,300 full load
Dimensions, feet *(metres)*	337·9 × 47·6 × 15·7 (*103·0 × 14·5 × 4·8*)
Guns	4 57-mm AA (1 quadruple forward)
Mines	400
Main engines	4 diesels; 2 shafts; 8,000 bhp
Speed, knots	20
Complement	150

"Amga" class
(*S. Breyer*)

In service since 1965. Fitted with 4 mine tracks to provide stern launchings. Also have a capability in general support role.

2 "Wilhelm Bauer" Class
(Submarine Tenders)

Kuban (ex-Waldemar Kophamel)
Pechora (ex-Otto Wünche)

Displacement, tons   4,726 standard; 5,600 full load
Dimensions, feet (*metres*) 446·0 × 52·5 × 14·5 (*136·0 × 16·0 × 4·4*)
Main engines   4 MAN diesels; 2 shafts; 12,400 bhp
Speed, knots   20

Former German. Launched in 1939. *Kuban* was salvaged in 1950–51 after being sunk in shallow water by bombing in WW II and was rehabilitated in 1951–57.

12 "Amur" Class
(Repair Ships)

Displacement, tons   6,000 full load
Dimensions, feet (*metres*) 377·3 × 57·4 × 18·0 (*115·0 × 17·5 × 5·5*)
Main engines   Diesels; 2 shafts

A new class of general-purpose depot ships built since 1969. Successors to the "Oskol" class. In series production at a rate of about two a year.

"Amur" class

10 "Oskol" Class
(Repair Ships)

Displacement, tons	2,500 standard; 3,000 full load
Dimensions, feet (*metres*)	295·2 × 39·4 × 14·8 (*90·0 × 12·0 × 4·5*)
Main engines	2 diesels; 2 shafts
Speed, knots	16

Three series: "Oskol I" class, well-decked hull, no armament; "Oskol II" class, well-decked hull, armed with 2 57-mm guns (1 twin) and 4 25-mm guns (2 twin); "Oskol III" class, flush-decked hull. General-purpose tenders and repair ships. Built from 1963 to 1970 in Poland.

Atrek
Ayat
Bakhmut
Dvina
Murmats
Osipov

6 "Atrek" Class
(Submarine Support)

Displacement, tons	3,500 standard; 6,700 full load
Measurement, tons	3,258 gross
Dimensions, feet (*metres*)	336 × 49 × 20 (*102·5 × 14·9 × 6·1*)
Main engines	Expansion and exhaust turbines; 1 shaft; 2,450 hp
Speed, knots	13
Boilers	2 water tube
Range, miles	3,500 at 13 knots

Built in 1956–58, and converted to naval use from "Kolomna" class freighters. There are six of these vessels employed as submarine tenders and replenishment ships. Some may have up to 6 37-mm (twins).

5 "Dnepr" Class
(Submarine Tenders)

Displacement, tons	4,500 standard; 5,250 full load
Dimensions, feet (*metres*)	370·7 × 54·1 × 14·4 (*113·0 × 16·5 × 4·4*)
Main engines	Diesels; 2,000 bhp
Speed, knots	12

Bow lift repair ships for S/M support and maintenance. Built in 1957–66 and equipped with workshops and servicing facilities. The last two ships of this class form the "Dnepr II" class.

"Dnepr II" class
(S. Breyer)
Tovda

1 "Tovda" Class
(Repair Ship)

Displacement, tons	3,000 standard; 4,000 full load
Dimensions, feet (*metres*)	282·1 × 39·4 × 16·0 (*86·0 × 12·0 × 4·9*)
Guns	6 57-mm AA (3 twin mountings)
Main engines	Triple expansion; 1,300 hp
Speed, knots	11

Polish built ex-tanker converted in 1958.

Intelligence Collectors

In the early 1960s NATO warships started reporting the presence of a number of Intelligence Collectors fitted with electronic interception gear in the vicinity of major exercises. In 1963 the *Gidrofon, Deflektor, Mukson* and *Olonec* had been identified – the forerunners of a considerable fleet of these craft which steadily spread throughout the world. There is no point in itemising the various classes into which this fleet, now of 54 ships, is split – that is done in the following section. Many are small ships whose trawler parentage is seen in the open starboard superstructure where the trawl was originally brought home. But the six ships of the "Primorye" class are far more impressive. These 5,000-ton ships carry not only a very comprehensive set of aerials but also what appears to be two transportable deck-houses, one on the bridge and the other abaft the funnel. It seems more than likely that these contain not only processing but possibly analysis equipment. Whatever the size of these ships, however, the presence of the AGIs must provide the Soviets with a vast mass of electronic data which, particularly in the event of careless use of equipment, allows a careful analysis to be made of Nato and other foreign electronic transmissions, radio, radar and ECM. Either in company with fleet units and task forces or stationed off the Polaris bases at the Clyde, Rota, Guam or Charleston these ships are a regular feature of every commander's plot today.

INTELLIGENCE COLLECTORS (AGIs)

6 "Primorye" Class

Displacement, tons   5,000
Dimensions, feet (*metres*) 274 × 45 × 26·2 (*83·6 × 13·7 × 8·0*)

Primorye
Kavkaz
Krym
Zabaikalye
Zaporozye
Zakarpatye

"Primorye" class
AGI *Zakarpatye*

The most modern intelligence collectors in the world, apparently with built-in processing and possibly, analysis capability. Hull design is that of the "Majakowsky" class fish-factory ships.

Alidada	*Linza*
Ampermetr	*Lotlin*
Barograf	*Reduktor*
Barometr	*Repiter*
Deflektor	*Teodolit*
Ekholot	*Traverz*
Gidrofon	*Zond*
Krenometr	

15 "Okean" Class

Measurement, tons   680 gross
Dimensions, feet (*metres*) 178 × 30·6 × 15·9 (*54·3 × 9·3 × 4·8*)
Main engines   Diesel; 1 shaft; 800 hp
Speed, knots   12

Built in USSR in 1965. Apparently identical to "Mayak" class – both have the same variations in the superstructure with the port side closed in and the starboard side open, a relic of their design as trawlers. In the last year at least four modified as shown.

INTELLIGENCE COLLECTORS

Left: "Modified Okean"
below: "Okean" class
Traverz

8 "Lentra" Class

GS 34
GS 36
GS 41
GS 43
GS 46
GS 47
GS 55
GS 59

Displacement, tons	250
Measurement, tons	334 gross; 186 deadweight
Dimensions, feet (*metres*)	143 × 25 × 12·5 (*43·6 × 7·6 × 3·8*)
Main engines	Diesel; 400 hp
Speed, knots	10·5

All built in USSR 1957–63. Now have names in addition to numbers. Two known as *Neringa* and *Izvalta*.

8 "Mayak" Class

Aneroid
Girorulevoy
Khersones
Kurs
Kursograf
Ladoga
GS 239
GS 242

Measurement, tons	680 gross; 252 net
Dimensions, feet (*metres*)	178 × 30·6 × 15·9 (*54·3 × 9·3 × 4·8*)
Main engines	Diesel
Speed, knots	13

Built in USSR 1965. Apparently identical to "Okean" class – see notes for that class.

4 "Mirny" Class

Bakan
Lotsman
Val
Vertikal

Displacement, tons	850
Dimensions, feet (*metres*)	208 × 31·2 × 13·8 (*63·4 × 9·5 × 4·2*)
Main engines	Diesel; 1 screw
Speed, knots	15

6 "Moma" Class

Arkepelag
Ilmen
Jupiter
Nakhodka
Pelorus
Seliger

Displacement, tons	1,240 standard; 1,800 full load
Dimensions, feet (*metres*)	219·8 × 32·8 × 13·2 (*67·0 × 10·0 × 4·0*)
Main engines	Diesels
Speed, knots	16

2 "Pamir" Class

Gidrograf
Peleng

Measurement, tons	2,000 gross
Dimensions, feet (*metres*)	256 oa × 42 × 13·5 (*78·0 × 12·8 × 4·1*)
Main engines	2 4-stroke diesels; 2 shafts; 4,200 bhp
Speed, knots	17

Built in Sweden 1959–60. Originally salvage tugs.

INTELLIGENCE COLLECTORS

Left: "Lentra" class
(Michael D. J. Lennon);
centre: "Mayak" class;
bottom: "Moma" class
AGI *Jupiter*
*(Commander Aldo
Fraccaroli)*

"Pamir" class
(S. Breyer)

Izmeritel
Protraktor

2 "Dnepr" Class

Measurement, tons   500 gross
Dimensions, feet (*metres*) 150 × 30 × 8 (*45·8 × 9·2 × 2·4*)
Main engines   Diesel
Speed, knots   11

Gidrolog

1 "T58" Class

Displacement, tons   900 full load
Dimensions, feet (*metres*) 229·9 × 29·5 × 7·9 (*70·1 × 9·0 × 2·4*)
Main engines   2 diesels; 2 shafts; 4,000 bhp
Speed, knots   18

Built in USSR 1962.

G. Sarychev
K. Laptev

2 "Zubov" Class

Displacement, tons   3,021 full load
Dimensions, feet (*metres*) 295·2 × 42·7 × 15 (*90·0 × 13·0 × 4·6*)
Main engines   Diesels; 2 shafts
Speed, knots   16·5 knots

Built in Poland 1975.

Survey and Research Ships

The Institute of Oceanology of the Academy of Sciences was established by a decree signed by Lenin on 10 March 1921. Since then it has grown into the highly complex organisation which is today centred in Moscow. In addition to the general study of the oceans four departments deal with (a) chemistry; (b) physics; (c) biology and geology; (d) equipment, computers and registration. Four main outstations are established at Kalingrad (the Atlantic section), Leningrad (overall oceanic flow), Gelendjuk (the Black and Mediterranean seas with a special responsibility for underwater work) and Vladivostok (Pacific and Indian Oceans). Fifteen separate institutes, all allied to the Institute of Oceanology, deal with specialised subjects such as acoustics (Moscow), hydrophysics (Sevastopol), computer studies (Novosibirsk), geophysics (Sakhalin), marine biology (Murmansk). Some thirty major ships and a considerable number of smaller ones now operate for the Institute.

The foregoing is a brief summary of a vast organisation. A second very considerable directorate comes under the charge of the Head of the Chief Directorate of Navigation and Oceanography of the Ministry of Defence and Head of the Hydrographic Service of the Navy, a post at present held by Admiral Rassokho. Under his direction are the hydrographic staffs of the four major fleets and 120 surveying ships of various sizes.

A separate organisation, the Department of Marine Forecasting, a branch of the USSR Hydrometeorological Research Centre in Moscow, combines the data received from not only the research and surveying ships but also from satellites, fishery research ships, fishing and merchant ships, as well as a large network of shore stations. The resulting forecasts are available to all Soviet ships and aircraft with an additional facility for re-routing ships past areas of heavy weather.

The third group of specialised research ships are those working for the space-programme, the "Space Associated" ships. The twenty-five vessels assigned this task are dealt with in detail in the following pages as are the fourth category, the fishery-research ships. Of these, at least 193 of varying sizes are operational world-wide using highly specialised

179

equipment ranging from a pair of converted submarines, free-ranging automated underwater vehicles to modern deep-water trawls.

Of the ships involved in these many tasks the fore-runner was the 500-ton *Persei* which was cobbled together at Archangel in 1922–23 for the new Institute of Oceanology. With a wooden schooner's hull, engines salved from a wreck and other equipment from various scrapyards her record of 84 research voyages in her twenty years of life is as surprising as it is unique. She was the Soviet's only pre-war research ship totally dedicated to the task, although others were taken up temporarily for various operations, particularly the twenty-seven Russian expeditions of the 1932–33 International Polar Year.

In 1945 the Institute's fleet was back to zero – then came the most famous of them all, *Vityaz*, a conversion of a 5,700-ton German fruit carrier. She was followed by the 600-ton wooden auxiliary sailing ship *Zarya*, which, since her completion in 1952, has logged nearly a quarter of a million miles devoted to geomagnetic research. From this time on matters moved apace. In the International Geophysical Year (1957) a quarter of the eighty ships involved were Soviet vessels – in the Global Atmospheric Research Programmes' Atlantic Tropical Experiment (GATE), (June–September 1974), of the international fleet of thirty-seven ships from ten countries a third came from the USSR. This has been made possible by a very large building and conversion programme – *Mikhail Lomonosov*, the inseparable pair *Vavilov* and *Lebedev*, *Shokalsky* and *Voiekov*, the first ships with long-range meteorological rockets, the "Akademik Kurchatov" class and their successors – so that today, as we have seen, no less than thirty of these ships are deployed world-wide.

The main bulk of the present hydrographic fleet of 120 ships dates from the 1960s – Admiral Gorshkov's determination to get his fleet to sea needed those vital precursors, the surveying ships. Although a huge purchasing programme of foreign, particularly British, charts was in full swing and continues today, special tasks such as bottom-contouring needed special ships to execute them. Where the fleet is to go the surveyors must lead and if, as in the Soviet case, the operating area is to be the world the hydrographic task becomes a global one. The twenty-two "Momas", nineteen "Kamenkas" and "Biyas", the sixteen "Samaras", five "Telnovsks", eleven "Malygins", nine "Nikolai Zubovs" and some forty other vessels make up the fleet of 120 – a considerable slice of the world-wide total of 320 naval survey ships and craft.

From the four organisations operating a total of 368 ships at sea a vast store of data flows back to the Soviet Union. There can be little doubt that the Soviet Navy is today as well provided with operational information – hydrographic, acoustic, submarine, A/S, meteorological – as any fleet has ever been. Although there are some suggestions that more modern techniques could be adopted, the sheer volume of knowledge is there and this all comes from a fleet of survey and research ships built up in the last twenty years.

SURVEY SHIPS

24 "Moma" Class (+6 AGIs)

Displacement, tons	1,240 standard; 1,500 full load
Dimensions, feet (*metres*)	240 × 36·3 × 9·6 (*73·2 × 11·1 × 2·9*)
Main engines	Diesels
Speed, knots	17

Eight ships of this class were reported to have been built from 1967 to 1970 and the remainder since. Naval manned.

9 "Kamenka" Class
10 "Biya" Class

Displacement, tons	750 standard; 1,000 full load
Dimensions, feet (*metres*)	180·5 × 31·2 × 11·5 (*55·1 × 9·5 × 3·5*)
Main engines	Diesels
Speed, knots	16
Range, miles	4,700 at 11 knots
Endurance	15 days

The ships of these classes are not named but have a number with the prefix letters "GS". All reported to have been built since 1967–68. Naval manned.

4 "Telnovsk" Class

Displacement, tons	1,200 standard
Measurement, tons	1,217 gross, 448 net
Dimensions, feet (*metres*)	229·6 × 32·8 × 13·1 (*70·0 × 10·0 × 4·0*)
Main engines	Diesels
Speed, knots	10

Formerly coastal freighters. Built in Bulgaria and Hungary. Refitted and modernised for naval supply and surveying duties. Naval manned. Sister ship *Stvor* appears under Training Ships.

Altair   *Krilon*
Anadir   *Kolguev*
Andromeda   *Liman*
Antares   *Mars*
Anton Ktyda   *Morsoviec*
Arktika   *Okean*
Askold   *Pelorus*
Berezan   *Rybachi*
Cheleken   *Sever*
Ekvator   *Taymyr*
Elton   *Vega*
Kildin   *Zapolara*

Aytador
Gromova
Ulya
Sviyaga

"Kamenka" class

Izumrud (Michael D. J. Lennon)

Izumrud

Measurement, tons	3,862 gross; 465 net
Main engines	Powered by diesel-electric machinery

A new type of research and survey ship built in 1970. Civilian manned.

Azimut   *Tropik*
Deviator   *Zenit*
Gidrolog   *Vagach*
Gigrometr   *Vostok*
Globus   *Yug*
Glubomer
Gorizont
Gradus
Kompas
Pamyat Merkuryia
Rumb

16 "Samara" Class

Displacement, tons	800 standard; 1,200 full load
Measurement, tons	1,276 gross; 1,000 net
Dimensions, feet (*metres*)	198 × 36·3 × 10·8 (*60·4 × 11·1 × 3·3*)
Main engines	Diesels
Speed, knots	16
Range, miles	6,200 at 11 knots

Built at Gdansk, Poland since 1962 for hydrographic surveying and research. Naval manned.

"Samara" class *Globus*
(Michael D. J. Lennon)

Akademik Kovalevsky
Akademik Vavilov

Measurement, tons   284 gross (*Vavilov* 255)
Dimensions, feet (*metres*) 126·8 × 23·7 × 11·5 (*38·1 × 7·2 × 3·5*)
                    (*Vavilov* 119·7 × 24·1 × 11·5) (*36·5 × 7·4 × 3·5*)
Main engines   1 diesel
Speed, knots   10

Built in E. Germany in 1949.

Akademik Arkhangelsky

Measurement, tons   416 tons gross
Dimensions, feet (*metres*) 132·9 × 25 × 13 (*40·5 × 7·6 × 4·0*)
Main engines   1 diesel
Speed, knots   10

Built in USSR in 1963.

Right: *Akademik Kovalevsky*; below *Akademik Archarpelsky* (Michael D. J. Lennon)

Mgla

Measurement, tons	299 gross
Dimensions, feet (*metres*)	129·5 × 24·3 × 11·8 (*39·5 × 7·4 × 3·6*)
Main engines	1 diesel
Speed, knots	8·5

11 "Dmitri Ovstyn" Class

A. Smirnov
Dmitri Laptev
Dmitri Ovstyn
Dmitri Sterlegov
E. Toll
N. Kolomeytsev
*N. Yevgenov**
*S. Krakov**
Stefan Malygin
Valerian Albanov
*V. Sukhotsky**

Displacement, tons	1,800 full load
Dimensions, feet (*metres*)	220 × 39 × 15 (*67·1 × 11·9 × 4·6*)
Main engines	Diesels; 2,000 bhp
Speed, knots	16

Built by Turku, Finland. Launched 1970–72. Civilian manned. Employed largely on geological research and survey in the Arctic. Last three, marked *, completed January to August 1974.

184

Mikhail Lomonosov

Displacement, tons	5,960 normal
Measurement, tons	3,897 gross; 1,195 net
Dimensions, feet (*metres*)	336·0 × 47·2 × 14·0 (*102·5 × 14·4 × 4·3*)
Main engines	Triple expansion: 2,450 ihp
Speed, knots	13

Built by Neptune, Rostock, in 1957 from the hull of a freighter of the "Kolomna" class. Operated not by the Navy but by the Academy of Science. Equipped with 16 Laboratories. Carries a helicopter for survey. Civilian manned.

9 "Nikolai Zubov" Class

A. Chirikov
A. Vilkitsky
Boris Davidov
F. Litke
Nikolai Zubov
S. Chelyuskin
Sejmen Dezhnev
T. Bellinsgausen
V. Golovnin

Displacement, tons	2,674 standard; 3,021 full load
Dimensions, feet (*metres*)	295·2 × 42·7 × 15 (*90·0 × 13·0 × 4·6*)
Main engines	2 diesels
Speed, knots	16·7 knots
Complement	108 to 120, including 70 scientists
Range, miles	11,000 at 14 knots
Endurance	60 days

Oceanographic research ships built at Szczecin Shipyard, Poland in 1964. *Nikolai Zubov* visited London in 1965. Employed on survey in the Atlantic. Naval manned.

Mgla (Michael D. J. Lennon)

Dolinsk

Measurement, tons   10,826 deadweight; 5,419 gross, 2,946 net
Dimensions, feet (*metres*) 456·0 × 58·0 × 15·5 (*139·0 × 17·7 × 4·7*)
Main engines   2 diesels

Built at Abo in Finland in 1959. Converted for surveying. Naval manned.

Zarya

Measurement, tons   71 net; 333 gross

Built in 1952 for geomagnetic survey work. Civilian manned.

Nerey
Novator

Measurement, tons   369 gross
Dimensions, feet (*metres*) 118·1 × 24·7 × 11·5 (*36·0 × 7·5 × 3·5*)
Main engines   2 diesels
Speed, knots   11

Built in USSR in 1956 and 1955. Originally fleet tugs of the "G" class. Converted for research. Civilian manned.

Opposite: *Mikhail Lomonsov*; below: *Dolinsk*; left: *Zarya*
(*Michael D. J. Lennon*)

187

Petrodvorets (ex-Bore II)

Measurement, tons	1,965 gross; 985 net
Dimensions, feet (*metres*)	254·2 × 39·4 × 24·9 (*77·5 × 12·0 × 7·6*)
Main engines	Diesel
Speed, knots	13·5

Built at Abo, Finland for Finnish owners in 1938. Sold to USSR in 1950 and renamed.

Zvezda

Measurement, tons	348 gross
Dimensions, feet (*metres*)	129 × 24·2 × 11·4 (*39·3 × 7·4 × 3·5*)
Main engines	Diesel
Speed, knots	10

Built in East Germany in 1957. Carries winches in the chains on the quarters. Sister ships *Zarnitsa* and *Yug* are used for transporting crews to ships building outside the USSR.

Nerey (Michael D. J. Lennon)

Paleh (ex-Bratsk)

Measurement, tons	2,285 gross; 987 net
Dimensions, feet (*metres*)	239·4 × 42·6 × 22 (*73·0 × 13·0 × 6·7*)
Main engines	1 diesel; 1 shaft
Speed, knots	11

Built in E. Germany in 1960 as fish-carrier of the "Evron" class. Converted for surveying and renamed in 1966.

Zvezda (Ian Brooke)

RESEARCH SHIPS

4 "Modified Akademik Kurchatov" Class

Abkhasia
Adzhariya
Bashkiriya
Moldavya

Displacement, tons	7,500 full load
Dimensions, feet (*metres*)	409·2 × 56 × 21·1 (*124·8 × 17·1 × 6·4*)
Main engines	2 diesels
Speed, knots	20·4
Range, miles	20,000 at 15 knots
Endurance, days	60

Fitted with helicopter platform aft. Naval manned. Completed in 1973.

7 "Akademik Kurchatov" Class

Akademik Korolev
Akademik Kurchatov
Akademik Shirshov
Akademik Vernadsky
Dmitri Mendeleyev
Professor Zubov
Professor Vize

Displacement, tons	6,681 full load
Measurement, tons	1,387 net; 1,986 deadweight; 5,460 gross
Dimensions, feet (*metres*)	400·3 to 406·8 × 56·1 × 15·0 (*122·1 to 124·1 × 17·1 × 4·6*)
Main engines	2 Halberstadt 6-cylinder diesels; 2 shafts; 8,000 hp
Speed, knots	18 to 20

All built by Mathias Thesen Werft at Wismar, East Germany between 1965 and 1968. All have a hull of the same design as the "Mikhail Kalinin" class of merchant vessels. There are variations in mast and aerial rig. *Professor Vize* is similar to *A. Shirshoy* whilst *A. Kurchatov*, *A. Vernadsky* and *D. Mendeleyev* are the same. Civilian manned.

Above: Modified "Akademik Kurchatov" class *Bashkirya*; right: "Akademik Kurehatov" class *Professor Vize* (Michael D. J. Lennon)

9 "Passat" Class

Measurement, tons   32,800 gross
Dimensions, feet *(metres)* 280 × 43 × 15·5 *(85·4 × 13·1 × 4·7)*
Main engines   Diesels; 4,800 hp
Speed, knots   16

Research or weather ships built at Szczecin, Poland, since 1968.

*Ernst Krenkel
  (ex-Vikhr)
Georgi Ushakov
  (ex-Schkval)
Musson
Okean*   *Poriv
Passat*   *Priliv
Priboi*   *Volna*

2 "Lebedev" Class

Measurement, tons   1,180 net, 3,561 gross
Main engines   Diesels

Research vessels with comprehensive equipment and accommodation. Both built in 1954.

*Petr Lebedev
Sergei Vavilov*

Vityaz (ex-Mars)

Displacement, tons   5,700 standard
Main engines   Diesels; 3,000 bhp
Speed, knots   14·5 knots
Range, miles   18,400 at 14 knots
Complement   137 officers and men including 73 scientists

Oceanographic research ship. Formerly a German freighter built at Bremen in 1939. Equipped with 13 laboratories.

"Lebedev" class *Petr Lebedev (J. A. Verhoog)*

"Modified Dobinya
Nikitich" class
Vladimir Kavrasky

Vladimir Kavrasky

1 "Modified Dobinya Nikitich" Class

Displacement, tons   2,500 standard
Dimensions, feet (*metres*) 223·1 × 59·1 × 18·1 (*68·0 × 18·0 × 5·5*)
Main engines   3 shafts
Speed, knots   13·8 knots

One of a numerous class of icebreakers built at Leningrad in the early 1960s –
converted for polar research in 1972.

Nevelskoy

1 "Nevelskoy" Class

Last of a class of three research ships.

Akademik Iosif Orbeli
Professor Nikolai Barabski
Akademik S. Vavilov

3 "Orbeli" Class

Built in Warnemünde 1969–71. Act as Supply Ships. Civilian manned.

3 "Polyus" Class

Baikal
Balkhash
Polyus

Displacement, tons	6,700 standard
Dimensions, feet (*metres*)	365·8 × 46·2 × 20·7 (*111·6 × 14·1 × 6·3*)
Main engines	Diesel-electric; 3,400 hp
Speed, knots	14
Range, miles	23,000 at 12 knots
Endurance	75 days

These ships of the "Polyus" class were built in East Germany in 1961–64. Oceanographic research ships.

Left: "Polyus" class
Polyus; below: *Vladmir
Obruchev (Michael D. J.
Lennon)*

Vladimir Obruchev

Measurement, tons	534 gross
Dimensions, feet (*metres*)	137·8 × 30·9 × 16·4 (*42·0 × 9·4 × 5·0*)
Main engines	2 diesels
Speed, knots	11

One of the "G" class tugs built in Romania in 1959 and subsequently converted for research duties.

FISHERY RESEARCH SHIPS

Akademik Knipovich
Professor Deryugin
Akademik Berg
Poseidon

4 BMRT Type

Measurement, tons	3,165 gross; 1,166 net
Dimensions, feet (*metres*)	277·8 × 46 × 32·9 (*84·7 × 14·0 × 10·0*)
Main engines	1 diesel
Speed, knots	13

Akademik Knipovich
(*Michael D. J. Lennon*)

Built as fishery research ships 1963–74. Civilian manned.

194

2 BMRT Type

Yu. M. Shokalsky
A. I. Voyeyvkov

Measurement, tons	3,200 gross
Dimensions, feet (*metres*)	278 × 46 × 33 (*84·8 × 14·0 × 10·0*)
Main engines	1 diesel
Speed, knots	13

Sister ships of BMRT-type fish-factory ships with freezer plant removed.
Survey ships registered at Vladivostok and operated in the Pacific. Completed
in 1959 at Nikolayev.

2 Atlantik Type

Gerakl
Professor Mesyatsyev

Measurement, tons	2,242 gross
Dimensions, feet (*metres*)	270 × 45 × 25 (*82·4 × 13·7 × 7·6*)
Main engines	2 8-cyl Karl Liebnecht diesels
Speed, knots	13

Modified "Atlantik" type stern-trawler fish-factory ships built at Stralsund,
E. Germany in 1972.

East German trawler
Okeanograf (Michael
D. J. Lennon)

Issledovatel
Tamango

2 Soviet "Trawler" Type

Measurement, tons   680 gross
Dimensions, feet (*metres*) 178 × 30·6 × 15·9 (*54·3 × 9·3 × 4·8*)
Main engines   1 diesel
Speed, knots   12

Apparently identical, except for aerials, to "Okean" and "Mayak" class AGIs. Have same different appearance of port and starboard sides of the superstructure, the former being closed in and the latter open.

Aysberg
Okeanograf
Poliarnik

3 East German Trawler Type

Measurement, tons   265 gross
Dimensions, feet (*metres*) 126·3 × 23·6 × 11·5 (*38·5 × 7·2 × 3·5*)
Main engines   1 diesel
Speed, knots   9·5

Opposite: Kosmonaut Yuri Gagarin (Michael D. J. Lennon); below: Kosmanaut Vladimir Komanov (J. van der Worde)

Built in East Germany 1952–56. Civilian manned. Rigging of foremasts varies in different ships.

Note: There are also at least 180 other ships and craft, mainly of smaller size, employed on Soviet fishery research.

SPACE ASSOCIATED SHIPS

Note: All civilian manned except "Baskunchak" class.

1 "Gagarin" Class

Kosmonaut Yuri Gagarin

Displacement, tons   45,000
Measurement, tons   32,291 gross; 5,247 net
Dimensions, feet (*metres*) 757·9; 773·3 oa × 101·7 × 30·0 (*231·2; 235·9* oa
                        × *31·0* × *9·2*)
Main engines   2 geared steam turbines; 1 shaft; 19,000 shp
Speed, knots   17

Design based on the "Sofia" or "Akhtubu" (ex-"Hanoi") class steam tanker. Built at Leningrad in 1970, completed in 1971. Used for investigation into conditions in the upper atmosphere, and the control of space vehicles. She is the largest Soviet research vessel. Has bow and stern thrust units for ease of berthing. With all four aerials vertical and facing forward she experiences a loss in speed of 2 knots.

Kosmonaut Vladimir Komarov (ex-Genichesk)

1 "Komarov" Class

Displacement, tons	17,500 full load
Measurement, tons	8,000 approximately
Dimensions, feet (*metres*)	510·8 × 75·5 × 29·5 (*155·8 × 23·0 × 9·0*)
Main engines	Diesels; 2 shafts; 24,000 bhp
Speed, knots	22

She was launched in 1966 at Nikolayev as *Genichesk* and operated as a merchant ship in the Black Sea for about six months. Converted to her present role at Leningrad in 1967. The ship is named in honour of the Soviet astronaut who died when his space craft crashed in 1967.

Akademik Sergei Korolev

1 "Korolev" Class

Displacement, tons	21,250
Measurement, tons	17,114 gross; 2,185 net
Dimensions, feet (*metres*)	597·1 × 82·0 × 30·0 (*182·1 × 25·0 × 9·2*)

Akademik Sergei Korolev (Michael D. J. Lennon)

Built at Nikolayev in 1970, completing in 1971. Equipped with the smaller type radome and two "saucers".

1 "Bezhitsa" Class

Bezhitsa

Measurement, tons	11,089 gross; 12,727 deadweight
Dimensions, feet (*metres*)	510·4 × 67·7 × 40·4 (*155·7 × 20·6 × 12·3*)
Main engine	Diesel
Speed, knots	17·5

Former freighter of "Poltava" class launched at Nikolayev in 1964, and subsequently completed as a research ship. The aerial horns were fitted in 1971. Directional aerials similar to those in *Dolinsk* and *Ristna* fitted on crane stowage forward of the bridge.

Bezhitsa (Michael D. J. Lennon)

4 "Sibir" Class

Chukotka
Sakhalin
Sibir
Suchan

Displacement, tons	4,000 standard; 5,000 full load
Measurement, tons	3,767 gross (*Chukotka* 3,800; *Suchan* 3,710)
Dimensions, feet (*metres*)	354 × 49·2 × 20 (*108·0 × 15·0 × 6·1*)
Guns	6 45-mm AA; 2 MG
Main engines	Triple expansion; 2 shafts; 3,300 ihp
Speed, knots	15
Range, miles	3,300 at 12 knots

Converted bulk ore carriers employed as Missile Range Ships in the Pacific. *Sakhalin* and *Sibir* have three radomes forward and aft, and carry helicopters. *Suchan* is also equipped with a helicopter flight deck. Launched in 1957–59. Formerly freighters of the Polish "B 31" type. Rebuilt in 1958–59 as missile range ships in Leningrad.

7 "Baskunchak" (ex-Vostok) Class

Apsheron (ex-Tosnoles)
Baskunchak (ex-Vostok 4)
Dauriya (ex-Suzdal)
Dikson (ex-Vagales)
Donbass (ex-Kirishi)
Sevan (ex-Vyborgles)
Taman (ex-Vostok 3)

Measurement, tons	2,215 net; 6,450 deadweight; 4,896 gross
Dimensions, feet (*metres*)	400·3 × 55·1 × 14·0 (*122·1 × 16·8 × 4·3*)
Main engines	B & W 9-cylinder diesels
Speed, knots	15

Standard timber carriers modified with helicopter flight-decks. Built at Leningrad between 1963 and 1966. Entirely manned by naval personnel.

Borovichi (ex-Svirles)
Kegostrov (ex-Taimyr)
Morzhovets
Nevel

4 "Morzhovets" (ex-Vostok) Class

Former timber carriers but completely modified with a comprehensive array of tracking, direction finding and directional aerials. Additional laboratories built above the forward holds. Same measurements as the "Baskunchak" class, but tonnage increased to 5,277 gross and 967 net.

Chazhura
  (ex-Dangara)
Dshankoy
Chumikan
  (ex-Dolgeschtschelje)

3 "Dshankoy" Class

Displacement, tons	5,300 light; 14,065 full load
Dimensions, feet (*metres*)	457·7 × 59·0 × 25·9 (*139·6 × 18·0 × 7·9*)
Aircraft	1 helicopter
Main engines	2 7-cyl diesels
Speed, knots	18

Formerly bulk ore-carriers of the "Dzankoy" class (7,265 tons gross). Soviet Range Instrumentation Ships (SRIS). Active since 1963.

Ristna

Measurement, tons	1,819 net; 4,200 deadweight; 3,724 gross
Dimensions, feet (*metres*)	347·8 × 47·9 × 14·0 (*106·1 × 14·6 × 4·3*)
Main engines	MAN 6-cylinder diesels
Speed, knots	15

Converted from a timber carrier. Built in East Germany at Rostok by Schiffs-werft Neptun in 1963. Painted white. Fitted with directional aerials on top of bridge wings. Served as Missile Detection Ship.

"Baskunchak" class
Taman (Michael D. J. Lennon)

Left: "Morzhovets"
class *Nevel*; below:
*Ristna (Michael D. J.
Lennon)*

COMMUNICATIONS RELAY SHIPS

20 "Libau" Class

Displacement, tons   310 standard; 380 full load
Dimensions, feet (*metres*) 170·6 × 21·5 × 9·0 (*52·0 × 6·6 × 2·7*)
Main engines   3 diesels; 2 shafts; 3,300 bhp
Speed, knots   24
Range, miles   1,500 at 12 knots

Note: Four new 6,000 ton cable ships ordered from Wártsilá, two in 1972/73
and two on 16 July 1974. *Katyn*, first of class, launched 20 Mar 1974.

Donetz
Ingul
Tsna
Yana
Zeya

CABLE LAYERS

5 "Klasma" Class

Displacement, tons	6,900
Measurement, tons	3,400 deadweight; 6,000 gross
Dimensions, feet (*metres*)	427·8 × 52·5 × 17 (*130·5 × 16·0 × 5·2*)
Main engines	5 Wártsilá Sulzer diesels; 4,950 shp
Speed, knots	14
Complement	118

Ingul and *Yana* were built by Wártsilá, Helsingforsvarvet, Finland, laid down on 10 October 1961 and 4 May 1962 and launched on 14 April 1962 and 1 November 1962 respectively. *Donetz* and *Tsna* were built at the Wártsilá, Abovarvet, Abo. *Donetz* was launched on 17 December 1968 and completed 3 July 1969. *Tsna* was completed in summer 1968. *Zeya* was delivered on 20 November 1970. *Donetz*, *Tsna* and *Zeya* are of slightly modified design.

"Klasma" class

Service Forces

This grouping includes, as will be seen from the following pages, impressive numbers of icebreakers, tugs and rescue ships which need little explanation. The main interest of this section lies in the comparatively late attention paid by the Soviets to the need for underway replenishment when their ships were far from base. In the initial deployments fuel was supplied by ordinary mercantile-design tankers, some of which were taken up from trade and, from time to time, exchanged for others of the same class. For instance, of the sixty "Altay" class tankers so far built, only six are definitely of naval attachment but this number could and is supplemented when required from commercial sources.

In 1971 the first specialised fleet replenishment ship, *Boris Chilikin*, was completed in Leningrad. She was based on a merchant tanker hull but was designed to carry not only 13,000 tons of fuel but also 400 tons each of ammunition, spares and victualling stores. Of 20,500 tons full load her speed of 16·5 knots is well below that considered necessary for the new generation of support ships in Western navies, but she and her two sisters have shown an appreciation of lessons learned in the early Soviet deployments to the Mediterranean. A smaller edition of *Chilikin*, the single 7,500-ton *Manych*, was completed in 1972 but has not so far been repeated. In line with this improvement in ships has come a great improvement in replenishment techniques. Whereas ten years ago slow or stopped fuelling astern was the normal method, today abeam replenishment under way in heavy weather is frequently employed.

SERVICE FORCES

Notes: (a) With the Soviet merchant fleet under State control any ships of the merchant service, including tankers, may be diverted to a fleet support role at any time. (b) Five 31,000-ton tankers (*Asheron, Grozny, Godermes, Makhachkaia* and *Mayrop*) currently building at Swan-Hunters for a Liberian firm could be used in Soviet naval operations.

Boris Chilikin
Dnestr
Vladimir Kolechitsky

3 "Chilikin" Class
(Fleet Replenishment Ships)

Displacement, tons	23,000 full load
Dimensions, feet (*metres*)	531·5 × 70·2 × 28·1 loaded (*162·1 × 21·4 × 8·6*)
Guns	4 57-mm (2 twin)
Main engine	Diesel; 9,900 hp; 1 shaft
Speed, knots	16·5 knots

Based on the "Veliky Oktyabr" merchant ship tanker design *Chilikin* was built at Leningrad, completing in 1971. This is the first Soviet Navy class of purpose built underway fleet replenishment ships for the supply of both liquids and solids, indicating a growing awareness of the need for afloat support for a widely dispersed fleet. Carries 13,000 tons fuel oil, 400 tons ammunition, 400 tons spares and 400 tons victualling stores.

"Chilikin" class *Dnestr*

1 "Manych" Class
(Fleet Replenishment Ship)

Displacement, tons   7,500
Guns   4 57-mm (2 twin) with *Muff Cob* radar

Completed 1972, probably in Finland. A smaller edition of the *Boris Chilikin* but showing the new interest in custom-built replenishment ships. The high point on the single gantry is very similar to that on *Chilikin's* third gantry.

1 "Sofia" Class
(Replenishment Tanker)

Akhtuba (ex-Khanoy)

Displacement, tons   45,000 full load
Measurement, tons   62,000 deadweight; 32,840 gross; 16,383 net
Dimensions, feet (*metres*) 757·9 × 101·7 × 32·8 (*231·2 × 31·0 × 10·0*)

Built as the merchant tanker *Khanoy* in 1963 at Leningrad, she was taken over by the Navy in 1969 and renamed *Akhtuba*. The hull type was used in the construction of the space associated ship *Kosmonaut Yuri Gagarin*.

Manych

Right: "Sofia" class
Akhtuba; below:
"Kazbek" class
(Michael D. J. Lennon)

Alatyr
Desna
Volkhov

3 "Kazbek" Class
(Replenishment Tankers)

Displacement, tons	16,250 full load
Measurement, tons	16,250 deadweight; 3,942 gross; 8,229 net
Dimensions, feet *(metres)*	447·4 × 63·0 × 23·0 *(136·5 × 19·2 × 7·0)*
Main engines	2 diesels driving single screw

Former "Leningrad" class merchant fleet tankers taken over by the Navy. Built at Leningrad and Nikolayev from 1951 to 1961. Seven others – *Karl Marx*, *Kazbek*, *Dzerzhinsk*, *Grodno*, *Cheboksary*, *Liepaya* and *Buguzuslan* have acted in support of naval operations. The original class numbered 64.

Radar. *Don 2.*

Left: "Altay" class
*Tarkhankut (Michael
D. J. Lennon)*; below:
"Uda" class *Lena*

6 "Altay" Class
(Support Tankers)

Altay
Elyenya
Izhora
Kola
Tarkhankut
Yegorlik

Displacement, tons 5,500 standard
Dimensions, feet (*metres*) 344·5 × 49·2 × 19·7 (*105·1 × 15·0 × 6·0*)
Main engines Diesels
Speed, knots 14

Building from 1867 onwards. By early 1975 over 60 of this class had been completed for naval and mercantile use.

6 "Uda" Class
(Support Tankers)

Dunay
Koida
Lena
Sheksna
Terek
Vishera

Displacement, tons 5,500 standard; 7,200 full load
Dimensions, feet (*metres*) 400·3 × 51·8 × 20·3 (*122·1 × 15·8 × 6·2*)
Main engines Diesels; 2 shafts; 8,000 bhp
Speed, knots 17

Koida has a beam fuelling rig on starboard side abaft bridge. Built since 1961.

"Pevek" class
(*Michael D. J. Lennon*)

Iman
Pevek
Olekma
Zolotoy Rog

4 "Pevek" Class
(Support Tankers)

Displacement, tons   4,000 standard
Measurement, tons   4,500 deadweight
Dimensions, feet (*metres*) 344·5 × 47·9 × 20·0 (*105·1 × 14·6 × 6·1*)
Main engines   Diesels; 2,900 bhp
Speed, knots   14

Part of a class of fifty merchant tankers built by Rauma-Repola, Finland between 1955 and 1966.

Konda
Rossosh
Soyanna
Yakhroma

4 "Konda" Class
(Support Tankers)

Displacement, tons   1,178 standard
Dimensions, feet (*metres*) 226·4 × 32·8 × 13·8 (*69·1 × 10·0 × 4·2*)
Main engines   1,100 bhp
Speed, knots   13

Cheremshan	*Lovat*
Indiga	*Orsha*
+4	*Seima*
Khobi	*Shacha*
Metan	*Shelon*
	Sosva
	Tunguska

15 "Khobi" Class
(Harbour Tankers)

Displacement, tons   800 light; 2,000 approx full load
Speed, knots   12 to 14

Built from 1957 to 1959.

Dora
Irtysh
Irbit

3 "Nercha" Class
(Harbour Tankers)

"Sura" class

SALVAGE VESSELS

1 "Nepa" Class

Karpaty

Displacement, tons   3,500 light; 5,000 standard
Dimensions, feet (*metres*) 410·1 × 52·5 × 16·4 (*125·1 × 16·0 × 5·0*)
Main engines   Diesels; 2 shafts

New type of submarine rescue and salvage ships similar to the "Prut" class but improved and enlarged and with a special high stern which extends out over the water for rescue manoeuvres. *Karpaty* completed 1969.

10 "Prut" Class

Altai
Breshtau
Zhiguili

Displacement, tons   2,120 standard; 3,500 full load
Dimensions, feet (*metres*) 296·0 × 36·1 × 13·1 (*90·3 × 11·0 × 4·0*)
Guns   2 25-mm
Main engines   Diesels; 4,200 bhp
Speed, knots   18

Large rescue vessels. Built since 1960.

9 "Sura" Class

Displacement, tons   3,150 full load
Dimensions, feet (*metres*) 285·4 × 48·6 × 16·4 (*87·0 × 14·8 × 5·0*)
Main engines   Diesels; 1,770 bhp
Speed, knots   13·2

Heavy lift ships built since 1965 in East Germany. Six built by 1972. Last, *Dioklas*, launched 21 February 1971.

LIFTING VESSELS

15 "Neptun" Class

Displacement, tons   700 light; 1,230 standard
Dimensions, feet (*metres*) 170·6 × 36·1 × 12·5 (*52·0 × 11·0 × 3·8*)
Main engines   Oil fuelled
Speed, knots   12

Similar to Western boom defence vessels, or netlayers. Built in 1957–60 by Neptun Rostock. Have a crane of 75 tons lifting capacity on the bow. One of this class is now based at Murmansk for the Maritime Fleet. She is acting as a diving vessel for hydrogeologists and construction personnel.

SUBMARINE RESCUE SHIPS

15 "Valday" Class
(ex-"T 58" Class)

Displacement, tons   725 standard; 850 full load
Dimensions, feet (*metres*) 222·1 × 29·9 × 7·5 (*67·7 × 9·1 × 2·3*)
Main engines   2 diesels; 2 shafts; 5,000 bhp
Speed, knots   20

Basically of similar design to that of the "T 58" class larger fleet minesweepers, but the hulls were completed as emergency salvage vessels and submarine rescue ships at Leningrad. Equipped with diving bell, decompression chamber, lifting gear and emergency medical ward. It has been reported that there may be an extra six smaller rescue ships based on the "T 43" hull. One transferred to India (*Nistar*).

TRANSPORTS

Kamchatka Mongol

2 "Lake" Class

Shim   *Olga*
Ob   *Shilka*
Ussurij (ex-Okhotsk)
Vishera

6 Coastal Type

Olga and *Ishim* are Coast Guard transports. *Ob* is 1,194-ton diesel-electric Antarctic support ship.

TORPEDO RECOVERY/PATROL BOATS

90 "Poluchat I" Class

Displacement, tons   100 standard
Dimensions, feet (*metres*) 98·4 × 19·7 × 5·9 (*30·0 × 6·0 × 1·8*)
Guns   2 25-mm (1 twin) or 2 MG (1 twin)

Employed as specialised or dual purpose torpedo recovery vessels and/or patrol boats. They have a stern slipway.

DISTILLATION SHIPS

10 "Voda" Class

Displacement, tons   2,100 standard
Dimensions, feet (*metres*) 267·3 × 37·7 × 14 (*81·5 × 11·5 × 4·3*)
Main engines   Diesels
Speed, knots   12

Water distillation ships built in 1956 onwards. No armament.

TRAINING SHIPS

Stvor

Displacement, tons   1,200 standard
Dimensions, feet (*metres*) 229·6 × 32·8 × 13·1 (*70·0 × 10·0 × 4·0*)
Main engines   Diesels
Speed, knots   10

Built in Hungary in late 1950s as a survey ship of the "Telnovsk" class. Now converted as a naval training ship with additional accommodation immediately forward of the bridge.

Note: None of the following ships is in the Navy List but their products are largely intended for the Navy.

Right: *Stvor*; below: "Zenit" class *Meridion*; opposite: "Professor Anichkov" class *Professor Khlyustin* (Michael D. J. Lennon)

Angara (ex-Hela)

Displacement, tons	2,115 standard; 2,500 full load
Dimensions, feet (*metres*)	323 × 42·5 × 11 (*98·5 × 13·0 × 3·4*)
Guns	2 4·1-in; 1 37-mm AA; 2 20-mm AA
Main engines	4 MAN diesels; 2 shafts; 6,300 bhp
Speed, knots	18
Range, miles	2,000 at 15 knots

Former yacht built by Stülcken, Hamburg. Launched in 1939. In the Black Sea.

Gorizont
Meridian
Zenit

3 "Zenit" Class

Measurements, tons	4,374 gross; 986 net
Length, feet (*metres*)	352·6 (*107·5*)
Beam, feet	47·2
Main engines	Two 8-cylinder diesels geared to one shaft

All were built in East Germany at Rostok by Schiffswerft Neptun in 1961–62. Mercantile Cadet Training but produces officers for the Navy.

2 "Sedov" Class

Kruzenstern
Sedov

Measurement, tons   3,064 gross

Barques. Built in 1921. Employed as sail training ship for midshipmen, cadets and junior seamen.

1 Ex-German Type

Tovarisch (ex-Gorch Foch)

Displacement, tons   1,350
Dimensions, feet (*metres*) 242·8 × 39·3 × 15 (*74·1 × 12·0 × 4·6*)
Sail area   19,350 sq ft
Guns   2 20-mm AA
Main engines   MAN diesel; 1 shaft; 520 bhp
Speed, knots   8
Oil fuel, tons   25
Range, miles   3,500 at 8 knots
Complement   260

Barque. Ex-German training ship. Built by Blohm & Voss, Hamburg. Launched in 1933. Of mercantile attachment but produces personnel for the Navy. Sail area 2,150 sq yds.

9 "Professor Anichkov" Class

Professor Anichkov
Professor Khlyustin
Professor Kudrevitch
Professor Minyayev
Professor Pavlenko
Professor Rybaltovski
Professor Shchyogolev
Professor Ukhov
Professor Yushcheko

Measurement, tons	5,993 gross; 1,512 net
Main engines	Diesels

Built at Szczecin, Poland between 1970–73. Used as training ships but can operate as store transports. *Professor Rybaltovski* has a series of square ports in place of the cutaway sections below the boat-deck.

10 Schooner Type

Enisej
Praktika (ex-Passat)
Tobol
Ucheba (ex-Mousson)
+6

Displacement, tons	300 approximately (ships vary)

Three masts. In the Baltic. Sailing vessels for training cadets, boys and volunteers. There are about ten three-masted schooners of 300 tons with one square sail on the foremast of the same class as the *Praktika* and *Ucheba*, built in Finland.

There are also the engineering training ships *Professor Kudrevitch*, *Professor Shchyogolev*, *Professor Yushchenko* and *Professor Aruchkov*, all built in 1970–71.

ICEBREAKERS

Note: The majority of these ships are operated by V/O Sudoimport – only a small number being naval manned.

1 Projected Large Nuclear Powered

Main engines	Nuclear reactors; steam turbines; 80,000 hp

Reported as in the design stage in October 1974.

2 Nuclear Powered

Arktika
Ledokoly

Displacement, tons	25,000 standard
Dimensions, feet (*metres*)	459 × 98·4 × 34 (*140·0 × 30·0 × 10·4*)
Aircraft	Helicopter with hangar
Main engines	2 nuclear reactors; steam turbines; 30,000 shp
Speed, knots	25

Building yard – Leningrad. *Arktika* launched summer 1973, started trials on 30 November 1974. Fitted with new type of reactor, the development of which may have retarded these ships' completion.

Lenin

1 Nuclear Powered

Lenin

Displacement, tons	16,000
Dimensions, feet (*metres*)	440 × 90·5 × 25 (*134·2 × 27·6 × 7·6*)
Aircraft	2 helicopters
Main engines	3 pressurised water-cooled nuclear reactors, 4 steam turbines; 3 shafts (no shaft in bow); 44,000 shp
Speed, knots	18
Complement	230

The world's first nuclear-powered surface ship to put to sea. Reported to have accommodation for 1,000 personnel. Built at the Admiralty Yard, Leningrad. Launched on 5 December 1957. Completed and commissioned on 15 September 1959.

The original reactors, prototype submarine variety, were replaced during refit at Murmansk 1966–72. The new reactors presumably have a longer core-life than the eighteen months of their predecessors. The turbines were manufactured by the Kirov plant in Leningrad. Three propellers aft, but no forward screw. Can maintain a speed of 3–4 knots in 8 ft ice, giving a path of some 100 ft.

3 "Ermak" Class

Ermak
Admiral Makarov
+ 1

Displacement, tons	20,241
Dimensions, ft (*m*)	442·8 × 85·3 × 36·1 (*135 × 26 × 11*)
Aircraft	2 helicopters
Main engines	9 Wártsilá-Sulzer (12-cylinder 12 ZH 40/48 diesels of 4,600 bhp each (total 41,400 hp) with Stromberg Ab generators feeding three Stromberg electric motors of total 36,000 shp; 3 shafts
Range, miles	40,000 at 15 knots
Speed, knots	19·5
Complement	115 plus 28 spare berths

The Soviet Union ordered three large and powerful icebreakers on 29 April 1970 from Wártsilá Shipyard, Helsinki, for delivery in 1974, 1975 and 1976. These are the largest diesel icebreakers in the world. Six Wártsilá auxiliary diesels, 7,200 bhp. Propelling and auxiliary machinery controlled electronically. These are the first vessels to be fitted with Wártsilá mixed-flow air-bubbling system to decrease friction between hull and ice. *Ermak* launched 7 September 1973 and completed 30 June 1974. *A. Makarov* laid down 10 September 1973 and launched 26 April 1974 for completion February 1975. Third unit laid down 9 July for launching March 1975 – completion possibly January 1976.

Ermak

Vladivostock
Kiev
Leningrad
Moskva
Murmansk

5 "Moskva" Class

Displacement, tons 12,840 standard; 15,360 full load
Dimensions, feet (*metres*) 368·8 wl; 400·7 oa × 80·3 × 34·5 (*112·5 wl; 122·2 oa × 24·5 × 10·5*)
Main engines 8 Sulzer diesel-electric; 3 shafts; 22,000 shp
Speed, knots 18
Oil fuel, tons 3,000
Range, miles 20,000
Complement 145

Built by Wártsilá Shipyard, Helsinki. *Moskva* was launched on 10 January 1959 and completed in June 1960. *Leningrad* was laid down in January 1959. Launched on 24 October 1959, and completed in 1962. *Kiev* was completed in 1966. *Murmansk* was launched on 14 July 1967, and *Vladivostock* on 28 May 1968. Designed to stay at sea for a year without returning to base. The concave embrasure in the ship's stern is a housing for the bow of a following vessel when additional power is required. There is a landing deck for helicopters and hangar space for two machines.

Eight generating units of 3,250 bhp each comprising eight main diesels of the Wártsilá-Sulzer 9 MH 51-type which together have an output of 26,000 electric hp. Four separate machinery compartments. Two engine rooms, four propulsion units in each. Three propellers aft. No forward propeller. Centre propeller driven by electric motors of 11,000 hp and each of the side propellers by motors of 5,500 hp. Two Wártsilá–Babcock & Wilcox boilers for heating and donkey work. *Moskva* has four pumps which can move 480 metric tons of water from one side to the other in 2 minutes to rock the icebreaker and wrench her free of thick ice.

Moskva

3 Shallow-water Type New Construction

Dimensions, ft (*m*)	185·3 × 51·5 × 13·8 (*56·5 × 15·7 × 4·2*)
Main engines	Diesel-electric; 3,400 shp; 2 shafts; 2 rudders
Speed, knots	14

Contract signed with Wártsilá. Helsinki on 22 March 1974 for the building of these three icebreakers for delivery in 1976. All to be fitted with Wártsilá air-bubbler system.

3 "Kapitan" Class

Kapitan Belousov
Kapitan Melechov
Kapitan Voronin

All built by Wártsilá Shipyard, Helsinki between 1954 and 1957. The ships have four screws, two forward under the forefoot and two aft.

Displacement, tons	4,375 to 4,415 standard; 5,350 full load
Dimensions, feet (*metres*)	265 wl; 273 oa × 63·7 × 23 (*80·8 wl; 83·3 oa × 19·4 × 7·0*)
Main engines	Diesel-electric; 6 Polar 8-cylinder; 10,500 bhp
Speed, knots	14·9
Oil fuel, tons	740
Complement	120

Afanasy Nikitin
Duran
Dobrinya Nikitich
Eroffrey Khabarov
Fedor Litke
Georgij Sedov
Ilya Muromets
Ivan Moskvitin
Ivan Kruzenshtern
Khariton Laptev
Peresvet
Petr Pakhtusov
Plug
Sadko
Semyon Dezhnev
Semen Chelyushkin
Vasily Poyarkov
Vasily Pronchishchev
Vladimir Rusanov
Yiriy Lisyansky
Vyuga

21 "Dobrinya Nikitich" Class

Displacement, tons	2,500 standard (average)
Measurement, tons	2,305 gross (ships vary)
Dimensions, feet (*metres*)	223·1 × 59·1 × 18·1 (*68·0 × 18·0 × 5·5*)
Main engines	3 shafts
Speed, knots	13·8

All built at Leningrad between 1961 and 1965. Divided between the Baltic, Black Sea and Far East.

Top: *Kapitan Belousov*; right: "Dobrinya Nikitich" class *Yiriy Lisyansky (Michael D. J. Lennon)*

218

2 "Sibir" Class

Sibir (ex-Yosif Stalin)
Mikoyan (ex-Otto
Schmidt)

Displacement, tons	11,000
Measurement, tons	4,866 gross
Dimensions, feet (*metres*)	335·8 pp; 351 oa × 75·5 × 22 (*1024·0 pp;*
	107·0 oa × 23·0 × 6·7)
Aircraft	1 helicopter
Main engines	Triple expansion with diesel electric propulsion
	for cruising; 3 shafts; 10,050 hp
Speed, knots	15·5
Boilers	9
Fuel, tons	4,000 coal; and diesel oil
Complement	142

Sibir was built at the Baltic Works, Leningrad, launched 14 August 1937 and completed in 1939. *Mikoyan* was built by Nikolayev, launched in 1938 and completed in 1939. Three aircraft and 1 catapult were included in the design. Both in the White Sea.

Krassin (ex-Swiatogor)

Displacement, tons	10,200
Main engines	13,500 hp
Speed, knots	15
Complement	160

Built in 1917 by Armstrongs, Newcastle. Converted 1953–58, helicopter dock fitted.

ARMED ICEBREAKERS

3 "Modified Dobrinya Nikitich" Class

Ivan Susanin
Vladimir Kavraysky
+1

Ivan Susanin

Of similar major characteristics to "D. Nikitich" class but lengthened by 80 feet and modified with new bridge structure, twin 76-mm forward, 2 30-mm Gatling guns aft and a helicopter platform. *V. Kavraysky* at present has no armament. Listed as Arctic Survey Ships (AGSB) *Susanin* in Far East, one in Northern Fleet and one in Baltic.

TUGS

Agatan
Aldan

2 "Pamir" Class

Measurement, tons	1,443 to 2,032 gross
Dimensions, feet (*metres*)	256 oa × 42 × 13·5 (*78·0 × 12·8 × 4·1*)
Main engines	Two 10-cylinder 4-stroke diesels; 2 shafts; 4,200 bhp
Speed, knots	17

220

Salvage tugs built at AB Gävie, Varv, Sweden, in 1959–60. Equipped with strong derricks, powerful pumps, air compressors, diving gear, fire fighting apparatus and electric generators.

"Pamir" class tug
Aldan

50 "Okhtensky" Class

Displacement, tons	835
Dimensions, feet (*metres*)	134·5 wl; 143 oa × 34 × 15 (*41·0 wl;* *43·6 oa × 10·4 × 4·6*)
Guns	1 3-in dp; 2 20-mm AA
Main engines	2 BM diesels; 2 electric motors; 2 shafts; 1,875 bhp
Speed, knots	14
Oil fuel, tons	187
Complement	34

Ocean-going salvage and rescue tugs. Fitted with powerful pumps and other apparatus for salvage. Pennant numbers preceded by MB.

50 Soviet Salvage Tugs

Measurement, tons   828 gross
Dimensions, feet (*metres*) 171·5 × 37·7 × 19 (*52·3 × 11·5 × 5·8*)
Main engines   Diesel-electric
Speed, knots   14

Built in late 1950s and early 1960s.

3 "Sorum" Class

Displacement, tons   approx 800
Length, feet (*metres*)   approx 160 (*48·8*)
Main engines   Diesels

A new class of ocean tugs first seen in 1973.

Finnish Salvage Tugs

Measurement, tons   1,070 gross
Dimensions, feet (*metres*) 201·2 × 39·2 × 18·1 (*61·4 × 12·0 × 5·5*)
Main engines   2 diesels
Speed, knots   14

Class of salvage and rescue tugs normally operated by Ministry of Fisheries with the fishing fleets. Built in Finland in late 1950s and early 1960s.

4 "Orel" Class

Displacement, tons   1,300
Main engines   Diesels
Speed, knots   11

Ocean-going tugs built between 1955 and 1958. Now being superseded.

7 "Katun" Class

Displacement, tons   950
Length, feet (*metres*)   210 (*64·0*)

Built in 1970–71.

Left: Soviet Salvage Tug *Atlant (Michael D. J. Lennon)*; centre: "Sorum" class tug; bottom: Finnish Salvage Tug *Stremitelny (Michael D. J. Lennon)*

15 "G" Class

Measurement, tons   534 gross
Dimensions, feet (*metres*) 156·5 × 32·2 × 16·4 (*47·7 × 9·8 × 5·0*)
Main engines   2 diesels
Speed, knots   11

Built in Romania in late 1950s. *Vladimir Obruchev* (see Research Ships) of same class.

Finnish "530 Ton" Class

Measurement, tons   533 gross
Dimensions, feet (*metres*) 157·1 × 31·3 × 15·5 (*47·9 × 9·5 × 4·7*)
Main engines   Steam
Speed, knots   9·5

Large class built in Finland in 1950s.

East German Berthing Tugs

Measurement, tons   233 gross
Main engines   Diesels

Large class built in 1970 in East Germany.

East German Harbour Tugs

Measurement, tons   132 gross
Dimensions, feet (*metres*) 94·5 × 21·3 × 9·8 (*28·8 × 6·5 × 3·0*)
Main engines   1 diesel
Speed, knots   10

Very large class built in E. Germany in 1964.

    There are a large number of other tugs available in commercial service which could be directed to naval use.

PART III

Soviet Naval Air Force (SNAF)

As is the case with the ships of the Soviet Navy the numbers of aircraft in the *Morskya Aviatsiya* have been reduced whilst their quality has been improved. At the time of Admiral Gorshkov's appointment in January 1956 the total of this force was being drastically pruned from some 4,000 aircraft manned and maintained by about 100,000 men. Of these at least half were fighter aircraft tasked with the protection of the ships engaged in the defence of the USSR. A breakdown of the present total of approximately 1,200 aircraft shows the changes in operational thought that have taken place in the last twenty years. Today the air-defence task is the responsibility of the Soviet Air Force – the SNAF is concerned primarily with reconnaissance, strike and ASW work.

The most numerous fixed-wing machines are the Tu-16 *Badgers* of which some 300 are equipped with *Kennel* (*Badger*-B), *Kipper* (*Badger*-C), *Kelt* or *Kerry* (AS6) (*Badger*-G) air-to-surface missiles whilst 55 are employed on reconnaissance duties, *Badger*-Ds being fitted with several search radars, *Badger*-Es with camera fittings and *Badger*-Fs with electronic pods under each wing. A few *Badger*-As with a free-fall bombing capability are believed to be in service still.

The largest aircraft of the SNAF inventory is the Tu-95 (Tu-20) *Bear* which, like the *Badger*, has been in service for twenty-one years. Some 50 *Bear*-Bs equipped with *Kangaroo* air-to-surface missiles form the strike element of this type, whilst the *Bear*-C and -D element is tasked with reconnaissance, missile targeting and missile guidance. The last of the *Bears* associated with naval operations, *Bear*-F, was first seen in 1973 with modified radar and additional stores bays, possibly an A/S version.

The third aircraft in this category is the *Blinder*, slightly larger than the *Badger*, of improved performance and first seen in 1961. This again appears in several versions, *Blinder*-A apparently only with the Air Force, *Blinder*-B in the maritime strike role with a single *Kitchen* air-to-surface missile and *Blinder*-C in a reconnaissance variant fitted with up to ten cameras and, apparently, Electronic Warfare (EW) equipment. Some 50 to 55 of these aircraft are estimated to be in service.

Where no estimate of numbers can be made is in the order-of-battle of the Tupolev *Backfire*, the first variable-geometry medium bomber in the SNAF. First reported in 1969, a larger aircraft than *Blinder* and capable of an action radius of 3,500 miles, *Backfire*-B will almost certainly replace the ageing force of twin-jet bombers. Currently armed with *Kitchen* and *Kerry* and later to carry a new 450-mile missile, this is a formidable addition to SNAF's strike capability.

In addition to the reconnaissance variants of the foregoing aircraft, all of which are capable of in-flight refuelling from converted *Badgers* and *Bisons*, the 75 Il-38 *Mays* provide a specialised A/S maritime patrol capability. With an under-slung radar, a magnetic anomaly detector (MAD) in the tail and a full load of sono-buoys and A/S stores this type is a conversion from the Il-18 *Coot* transport. Thus the basic design is nearly twenty years old but despite this and her reliance on four turboprops *May* appears to be an efficient and valuable aircraft. A shorter range maritime patrol aircraft is the Be-12 *Mail*, a twin turboprop amphibian which entered service in 1961. Some hundred of these are operational today and they are fitted with a nose radar and a MAD boom aft – a 10-ton payload can be carried, a formidable load in A/S warfare.

Also filling an important role in A/S operations are the helicopters of the Ka-25 *Hormone* type, which are rapidly replacing the older Mi-4 *Hound*. *Hormone*-A is the A/S version fitted with radar, a dunking sonar, A/S torpedoes and sono-buoys. These are now the standard embarked aircraft in cruisers and will, no doubt, provide a major part of *Kiev's* complement. The *Hormone*-B is a variant fitted for reconnaissance, target location and missile guidance.

Also a likely starter for the *Kiev's* complement is a development of the experimental Yak-36 *Freehand* VTOL aircraft first seen in 1967. Since then further trials have continued at Ramenskoye and at sea in *Moskva*.

Lastly in the order-of-battle come several hundred of the ever-necessary transport, training and utility aircraft, both fixed and rotary-wing.

Yak-36 *Freehand*

Crew	1
Engines	2 vectored-thrust turbojets (7,000–9,000 lb, 3,180–4,085 kg st each)
Dimensions	Span 27 ft (8·25 m), length overall 57 ft 6 in (17·5 m)
Speed	Approx Mach 0·85 at altitude
Range	Combat radius approx 175 miles (280 km)
Weight	Approx 18,000 lb (8,170 kg) loaded
Armament	2 16 unguided-rocket pods (wing pylons)

Yak-36 *Freehand (Tass)*

The Yak-36 is a Soviet V/STOL fighter aircraft, apparently developed for use aboard the Soviet Navy's aircraft carriers of the "Kuril" class. The single-seat, twin-engine aircraft has a barrel-like fuselage and swept wings similar to the MiG-15 and its derivatives. The aircraft has been observed operating from the Soviet helicopter cruiser *Moskva*.

First observed in July 1967, the Yak-36 has an elliptical cross section fuselage and employs two vectored-thrust turbojet engines for both vertical and horizontal thrust. This is the same arrangement used by the Hawker-Siddeley Harrier V/STOL aircraft. The aircraft also has a long in-flight refuelling probe protruding above the large, elliptical air intake.

Tupolev *Backfire*

Crew	2 to 4
Engines	2 Kuznetsov turbofans (40,000 lb + (18,160 kg) with afterburner)
Dimensions	Span 70 ft (21·35 m), length 130 ft (39·65 m)
Speed	Mach 2·0–Mach 2·5 at altitude
Ceiling	50,000 ft (15,250 m)
Range	2,750–3,570 miles (4,425–5,744 km) combat radius
Weights	270,000 lb + (122,580 kg) maximum
Armament	Air-to-surface missiles

The *Backfire* is a variable-geometry bomber entering service with Soviet Long-Range Aviation (LRA) and Naval Aviation and will probably replace the older *Badger* aircraft. With inflight refuelling it will have an intercontinental attack capability. The aircraft was first reported by US officials in 1969.

The outer portions of the *Backfire* wings extend for landing, take-off, and cruise flight, and swing back for high-speed flight; the aircraft has a conventional tail with a single tail fin. The two large turbofan engines have large, square air intakes and are believed to be based on the NK-144 turbofans that power the Tu-144 supersonic transport. The *Backfire* has a fixed refuelling probe in the nose. In the strike role the *Backfire* will probably carry long-range, air-to-surface missiles including the AS-6 *Kerry* and, possibly from 1976, a new 450-mile range ASM.

VARIANTS

Backfire-A probably initial development aircraft, large landing gear pods.

Backfire-B probably production aircraft; smaller landing gear pods.

Tu-16 *Badger*

Crew	Approx 7
Engines	2 Mikulin RD-3M (AM-3M) turbojets (19,180 lb, 8,708 kg st each)

Tu-16 *Badger*

Dimensions	Span 110 ft (33·50 m), length 121 ft (36·91 m) (*Badger*-C length 126 ft (38·43 m)), height 35 ft 6 in (10·83 m), wing area approx 1,820 sq ft (169·26 m²)
Speed	587 mph (945 km/hr) at 35,000 ft (10,675 m)
Ceiling	42,650 ft (13,008 m)
Range	3,000 miles (4,827 km) with full payload; 4,000 miles (6,435 km) with 6,600 lb (3,000 kg) bombs
Weight	158,600 lb (72,000 kg) maximum
Armament	7 23-mm cannon (except 6 23-mm cannon *Badger*-C/D) and 19,800 lb bombs (*Badger*-A; weapons bay)
	or 2 *Kennel* AS-1 ASMs (*Badger*-B)
	or 1 *Kipper* AS-2 ASM (*Badger*-C)
	or 1 *Kelt* AS-5 ASM (*Badger*-G)
	or 1 *Kerry* AS-6 ASM (*Badger*-G)

The Tu-16 *Badger* is a turbojet-powered medium bomber which has been in wide use by the Soviet Union for two decades and continues to serve in the conventional bomber, anti-ship missile, strategic and maritime reconnaissance, and tanker roles. The aircraft is also used by China, Egypt, Indonesia, Iraq, and Pakistan.

Tu-16 *Badger*

VARIANTS

Badger-A bomber aircraft with glazed nose; flown by Soviet LRA, Iraq,

Egypt (all 20 destroyed in June 1967).

Badger-B bomber aircraft with glazed nose; ASM capability; flown by Soviet LRA, Soviet Navy, Indonesia.

Badger-C bomber aircraft with nose radome; also used in maritime and strategic reconnaissance roles; ASM capability; flown by Soviet LRA, Soviet Navy.

Badger-D maritime reconnaissance aircraft with nose radome; small electronics blisters under fuselage; flown by Soviet Navy.

Badger-E reconnaissance aircraft similar to *Badger*-A with glazed nose; cameras fitted in weapons bay.

Badger-F reconnaissance aircraft similar to *Badger*-E with glazed nose; electronic pods fitted on wing pylons.

Badger-G bomber aircraft with glazed nose; ASM capability; flown by Soviet Navy, Egypt.

Badger-H/J/K reconnaissance aircraft.

Tu-95 (Tu-20) *Bear*

Crew	Approx 5
Engines	4 Kuznetsov NK-12 turboprops (14,795 ehp each, as uprated)
Dimensions	Span 159 ft (48·50 m), length 155 ft 10 in (over probe) (47·50 m), height 40 ft (12·19 m), wing area 3,000 sq ft (279 m²)
Speed	550 mph (885 km/hr) at 36,000 ft (11,000 m) (Mach 0·83); long-range cruise 440 mph (708 km/hr) at 36,000 ft (11,000 m) (Mach 0·67)
Ceiling	45,000 ft (13,715 m)
Range	7,800 miles (12,555 km) with 25,000 lb (13,338 kg) weapons carried to target; up to 9,000 miles (14,480 km) in reconnaissance role
Weight	340,000 lb (154,360 kg) maximum
Armament	1 20-mm or 23-mm cannon optional (nose mounting), up to 6 23-mm cannon (twin dorsal, ventral, tail turrets) and 25,000 lb (11,350 kg) nuclear or conventional bombs (weapons bay)
	or 1 *Kangaroo* AS-3 ASM (external)

The *Bear* is the only turboprop-propelled strategic bomber to enter operational service with any air force, and provides the Soviet Navy with some 50 long-range reconnaissance aircraft and a few anti-submarine aircraft. The *Bear* is a swept-wing aircraft with four wing-mounted turboprop engines turning counter-rotating propellers.

Tu-95 *Bear*

VARIANTS

Bear-A strategic bomber with glazed nose for bombardier; full gun armament.

Bear-B strategic bomber with radome under nose and faired blister on starboard side of after fuselage; in-flight refuelling capability; *Kangaroo* missile carried.

Bear-C reconnaissance variant of *Bear*-B with faired blisters on both sides of after fuselage.

Bear-D maritime reconnaissance variant with large belly radome; fitted for missile guidance; approx 8 crew; operational since 1965.

Bear-E reconnaissance variant of *Bear*-A with glazed nose, fixed refuelling probe, and camera openings in weapons bay position.

Bear-F maritime reconnaissance/anti-submarine aircraft; lengthened engine nacelles.

Tu-22 *Blinder*

Crew	3 or 4
Engines	2 turbojets (26,000 lb, 11,800 kg st each with afterburning)

Dimensions	span 90 ft 10½ in (27·70 m), length 132 ft 11½ in (40·53 m), height 17 ft (5·19 m)
Speed	920 mph (1,480 km/hr) at 40,000 ft (12,200 m) (Mach 1·4)
Ceiling	60,000 ft (18,300 m)
Range	1,250–1,350 miles (2,010–2,175 km) (later variants)
Weight	185,000 lb (84,000 kg) maximum
Armament	1 23-mm cannon (tail position) and 22,000 lb (9,988 kg) bombs (*Blinder*-A) or 1 *Kitchen* AS-4 ASM (*Blinder*-B)

The Tu-22 *Blinder* is a supersonic medium bomber flown by Soviet Long-Range Aviation (LRA) and Naval Aviation in the conventional bomber, anti-ship missile, maritime reconnaissance, and training roles. Although possibly intended as a successor to the *Badger*, only some 200 *Blinders* were built, most of which remain in service. The aircraft was first observed in June 1961.

The *Blinder* is a swept-wing aircraft with turbojet engines mounted in pods at the base of the tail fin; most aircraft have a partially retractable refuelling probe in the nose, a nose radome with small windows behind them in the lower fuselage, tandem seating for a three-man crew, fuel tanks faired into the wing trailing edges, and small wing tip pods.

VARIANTS

Blinder-A limited production bomber/reconnaissance aircraft.

Blinder-B bomber aircraft with ASM capability; enlarged nose radome.

Blinder-C maritime reconnaissance aircraft; 6 cameras fitted in weapons bay; presumably configured for electronic intelligence (ELINT).

Blinder-D Tu-22U; trainer with additional cockpit.

Be-12 *Mail*

Opposite: Tu-22 *Blinder*; left: Be-12 *Mail*

Crew	6 to 10
Engines	2 Ivchenko Al-20D turboprops (4,190 shp each)
Dimensions	Span 97 ft 6 in (29·70 m), length 99 ft (30·20 m), height 22 ft 11½ in (6·98 m)
Speed	379 mph (610 km/hr) at 10,000 ft (3,050 m); 200–250 mph (322–402 km/hr) cruise
Ceiling	37,000 ft (11,285 m)
Range	2,500 miles (4,023 km)
Weight	65,035 lb (29,525 kg) maximum
Armament	Various combinations of depth charges, torpedoes, mines, bombs (weapons bay and wing pylons)

The *Mail* is a twin turboprop-powered amphibian flown by the Soviet naval air arm. The Russian name for the aircraft is *Tchaika* (Seagull) and the designation is Be-12 or M-12, although the Nato code-name *Mail* is common in Western usage. The *Mail* was the direct successor of the Be-6 *Madge* in the Soviet naval air arm; the intermediate, jet-propelled Be-10 *Mallow* flying boat did not enter squadron service in the same manner as the contemporary Martin P6M Seamaster did not achieve US operational status. The *Mail* is slowly being replaced in service by the Il-38 *May* having been operational since 1961.

Il-38 *May*

Crew	Approx 12
Engines	4 Ivchenko Al-20M turboprops (4,250 shp each)
Dimensions	Span 122 ft 8½ in (37·40 m), length 129 ft 10 in (39·28 m), height 33 ft 4 in (10·17 m)
Speed	400 mph (64 km/hr) at sea level
Ceiling	35,500 ft (10,828 m)
Range	4,500 miles (7,240 km)
Armament	Various combinations of depth charges, torpedoes, bombs (weapons bay)

Il-38 *May*

The *May* is a four-turboprop maritime reconnaissance/anti-submarine aircraft being used in increasing numbers by the Soviet naval air arm. The *May* is a modification of the Il-18 *Coot* commercial airliner. *Mays* have flown from Egyptian bases with Russian crews but with UAR markings. The *May* has a longer fuselage than the *Coot* with a fixed radome under the nose, an internal weapons bay, and magnetic anomaly detector (MAD) boom fixed in the tail. An on-board computer is provided to perform tactical calculations.

Ka-25 *Hormone*

Crew	4
Engines	2 Glushenkov GTD-3 turboshafts (900 shp each)
Dimensions	Overall length 32 ft (9·76 m); height 17 ft 7½ in (5·37 m); main rotor diameters 51 ft 8 in (15·76 m)
Speed	137 mph (220 km/hr); 120 mph (193 km/hr) cruise
Ceiling	11,500 ft (3,508 m)
Range	400 miles (644 km)
Weights	9,700 lb (4,404 kg) empty; 16,100 lb (7,309 kg) maximum
Armament	2 ASW-torpedoes or nuclear depth charges

Ka-25 *Hormone*

The Ka-25 *Hormone* is a descendant of the earlier Kamov-designed Ka-15–Ka-18 series of piston-engine helicopters employed in large numbers in Soviet military and civilian activities. The *Hormone* is primarily a naval design, with an internal weapons bay for homing torpedoes and extensive ASW equipment. Submarine detection devices include radar in a chin housing, droppable sonobuoys, "dipping" magnetic anomaly detection (MAD), an electro-optical sensor in the tail and dunking sonar. The *Hormone*-B apparently has additional electronic equipment. Although dummy air-to-surface missiles were seen on an aircraft during a Soviet aviation day flight, no missiles are known to be operationally employed from the helicopter.

VARIANTS

Hormone-A standard utility and ASW variant.

Hormone-B special electronics variant.

Mi-4 *Hound*

Crew	2 + 16 troops
Engine	1 ASh-82V radial piston (1,700 hp)
Dimensions	Fuselage length 55 ft 1 in (16·81 m); height 17 ft (5·19 m); main rotor diameter 68 ft 11 in (21·01 m)
Speed	130 mph (209 km/hr); 100 mph (161 km/hr) cruise
Ceiling	18,000 ft (5,490 m) service
Range	155 miles (250 km)
Weight	17,200 lb (7,808 kg) maximum
Armament	1 MG (in forward fuselage and rockets on fuselage stations

Mi-4 *Hound*

Similar in basic configuration to its western contemporary, the Sikorsky H-19, the Mi-4 *Hound* is a transport and general purpose helicopter that entered Soviet service in 1953. Since that time, the *Hound* has become the most widely used Soviet rotary-wing aircraft, with several thousand having been built in both the Soviet Union and in China.

Soviet Naval Infantry

In the same way that the Royal Marines, the US Marine Corps and many other similar organisations extract a very high degree of esprit de corps from the demanding and frequently hazardous nature of their duties so the 12,000-strong Soviet Naval Infantry have found the same cohesion and enthusiasm. The operations of this force in the Great Patriotic War of 1941–45 were largely inhibited by the need to reinforce the army – over 400,000 sailors and infantry from the fleet were converted into land fighters. Despite the brilliance and success of a series of naval operations on the beaches of Southern Russia the results were apparently insufficient to call for the retention of the Naval Infantry in the post-war years. For some fifteen years, until the early 1960s, this force was in limbo. However, under the leadership of Admiral Gorshkov, well aware through his wartime experiences of the value of raiding and amphibious work, the preparations for this aspect of naval operations had already been put in hand. First in 1956–60 came the MP2 and MP4 classes of LCVs, small craft of some 800 tons to be followed in 1958 by the larger MP6 class of converted 2,000-ton merchant ships and the somewhat smaller MP8 class. Even smaller, and in many ways similar to the British LCT4, was the MP10 class, built between 1959–66. The craft were therefore available for local operations and in 1961–62 the Soviet Naval Infantry was re-established. With the force in being a new-construction programme of amphibious ships and craft was very soon in evidence. The first of these, the 1,000-ton "Polnocny" class LCTs, appeared in 1963 indicating that their design had been decided in 1959 at the latest. This thoroughness in planning was further shown when in 1965-66 the lead ship of the 5,800-ton "Alligator" class LSTs was built, to be followed a year later by the "Vydra" class LCVs of 500 tons. These building programmes have been continued until now twelve "Alligators", sixty "Polnocnys", thirty-five "Vydras" and the new class of "Ropucha" LCTs have joined the 46 more elderly amphibious craft.

In the last thirteen years the elite corps of the Naval Infantry has been built up to its present strength of 12,000. Each of the four main fleets includes a brigade of this force, further subdivided into ten battalions of 300–400 men. One of these is a tank battalion armed with thirty PT76 light tanks which are capable of amphibious landings. The infantry battalions are also mobile with a similar number of BTR60PB armoured personnel carriers which carry eight passengers and a crew of two and are armed with two machine guns.

During the last few years long-range deployments of the "Alligators" to Conakry, Cuba and the Indian Ocean have been reported while "Polnocnys" have been far afield in the Mediterranean. It appears that the Soviet amphibious forces are keeping well in line with the world-wide expansion of their surface, submarine and naval air forces. Backed by the 4,000-strong Sea Assault Regiment of the Polish Navy equipped with twenty-three "Polnocny" class LCTs, and with a very large amphibious-lift capability in the Soviet merchant marine this form of warfare allows the USSR a considerable range of options in both peace and war.

APPENDICES

SOVIET NAVAL MISSILES

Classification	System Number	Missile Code-name	Length ft	Launch wt lbs	Powerplant	Guidance	Range n miles	Mach Speed	Warhead	Launch Platforms	Notes
Strat	SSN-4	Sark	49·2	42,000 (est)	?2 stage solid	Inertial	300	—	Nuclear	Golf I, Zulu V submarines	Obsolescent. Operational 1958. Surface launched
Strat	SSN-5	Serb	35·0	40,000 (est)	2 stage solid	Inertial	700	—	Nuclear	Golf II and Hotel II submarines	Operational 1963. Surface launched
Strat	SSN-6	Sawfly	42·0	42,000 (est)	2 stage solid	Inertial	Mod 1 1,300 Mod 2 and 3 1,600	—	Nuclear (MRV in Mod 3)	Yankee submarines	Dived launch. Operational 1968 (Mod 1) 1974 (Mod 2 and 3)
Strat	SSN-8	—	45.0 (est)	45,000 (est)	2 stage liquid	Inertial	4,200	—	Nuclear	Delta and Delta II submarines. Hotel III for Trials	Dived launch. Operational 1972
SSM	SSN-1	Scrubber	22·5	9,000 (est)	Solid booster with turbojet sustainer	Radar/IR homing	130	0·9	HE	Krupny	Obsolescent. Operational 1958
SSM	SSN-2	Styx	15·0	5,500 (est)	2 stage solid	Active radar homing	23	0·9	HE	Osa I and Komars	2 Versions A and B. Operational 1960
SSM	SSN-3	Shaddock	42·0	26,000 (est)	2 boosters. Turbojet sustainer	Radar or IR with mid-course guidance	400 (max)	1·5	HE/ nuclear	Kynda, Kresta I, Juliet, Echo II, Whisky Long-Bin and Twin Cylinder	Operational 1961–62. In addition to mid-course guidance may be pre-programmed
SSM	SSN-7	—	22·0	—	—	—	30	1·5	—	Charlie, Papa	Dived launch. Operational 1969–70
SSM	SSN-9	—	30·0 (est)	—	—	Radar with mid-course guidance	150	1·0+	HE	Nanuchka	Operational 1968–69
SSM	SSN-10	—	25·0 (est)	6,000 (est)	—	Radar	29	1·2	—	Kara, Kresta II Krivak	Operational 1968
SSM	SSN-11	—	21·0	—	Probably as in SSN-2	?Radar probably	29	0·9	—	Osa II, mod Kildin mod Kashin	Probably mod SSN-2 with folding wings. Low altitude. Operational 1968

Classi-fication	System Number	Missile Code-name	Length ft	Launch wt lbs	Powerplant	Guidance	Range n-miles	Mach Speed	Warhead	Launch Platforms	Notes
SSM?	SSN-13	—	—	—	—	Inertial	400?	4·0?	Nuclear?	Possibly submarine	A new anti-ship/submarine weapon, probably with a ballistic trajectory
SAM	SAN-1	Goa	19·3	900 (est)	2 stage solid	Radio command	17	2·0	HE	SAM Kotlin, Kanin, Kashin, Kynda, Kresta I	Operation 1961
SAM	SAN-2	Guideline	34·7	5,000 (est)	Solid booster, Liquid sustainer	Radar homing	25	3·5	HE (290 lbs)	Dzerzhinski	Operational ?1954
SAM	SAN-3	Goblet	20·0	—	2 stage solid	—	20	—	HE	Kuril, Moskva, Kresta II	Operational 1967
SAM	SAN-4	—	—	—	—	—	20	—	HE	Kara, Krivak, Grisha, Nanuchka, Kril (?), Sverdlov	Operational 1969. May be unguided conversions
SAM	SAN-7	Grail	4·8	20 (est)	Solid boost with sustainer	IR homing	2	1·5	HE (5 lbs)	Osa I and II Shershen	
ASM	AS-1	Kennel	27·9	—	Turbojet	?Beam-rider	55	0·9	HE	Badger B	Obsolete
ASM	AS-2	Kipper	31·0	—	Turbojet	—	115	1·0+	HE	Badger C	Obsolescent. Operational 1960
ASM	AS-3	Kangaroo	49·2	—	Turbojet	—	400	1·5+	—	Bear B and C	Operational 1961
ASM	AS-4	Kitchen	37·0	—	1 stage liquid	?Inertial guidance	185	2·0+	—	Blinder B	Operational 1965
ASM	AS-5	Kelt	30·8	—	1 stage liquid	Active radar homing	120	0·9	—	Badger G	Operational 1968
ASM	AS-6	Kerry	32·0 (est)	—	1 stage liquid	—	?300	—	—	Badger (possibly Backfire)	Operational 1970

Note:
(a) A new ASM is reported under trials with a range of 450 n-miles and low-level capability probably to be carried by Backfire.
(b) SSC-2, Samlet is a coast defence version of AS-1, Kennel.

SOVIET NAVAL GUNS

Calibre in mm	Length in calibres	No. of barrels	Elevation	Rate of fire per barrel (rounds per minute)	Weight of shell (kg)	Range (metres) Surface	AA (slant)	Associated Radar/Director	Mounted in
152	50	Three per turret	50°	10	50	27,000 max 18,000 opt	—	Top Bow and Egg Cup	Sverdlov and Chapaev classes
130	50	Twin	40°	10	27	24,000 max 15,000 opt	—		Skory (unmod) class
130	58	Twin (semi-auto, dual purpose	50°	15	27	28,000 max 18,000 opt	13,000	Sun Visor and Egg Cup/ Wasphead	Skory (mod), Kotlin and Tallin classes
100	50	Twin (dual purpose)	80°	15	16	20,000 max 12,000 opt	15,000 max 9,000 opt	Top Bow/Post Lamp and Egg Cup	Sverdlov and Chapaev classes
100	50	Single (dual purpose)	40°	15	13·5	16,000 max 10,000 opt	6,000		Kola, Riga and Don classes
85	50	Twin (Skory) Single (Kronstadt)	70°	10	12	15,000 max 9,000 opt	6,000		Skory (some) and Kronstadt classes
76	60	Twin (dual purpose)	85°	60	16	15,000 max	14,000	Owl Screech	Kuril, Kara, Kynda Kashin, Krivak, Petya and Mirka classes
57	70	Twin or quadruple	85°	120/150	2·8	9,000	6,000	Hawk Screech	Don, Lama, Oskol, Tovda, Alligator, MP8, T58 classes (Twins). Kanin, Krupny and Lama classes (quads).

Calibre mm	Length in calibres	No. of barrels	Elevation	Rate of fire per barrel (rounds per minute)	Weight of shell (kg)	Range (metres) Surface	AA (slant)	Associated Radar/Director	Mounted in
57	80	Twin AA automatic	85°	120	2·8	12,000	5,000	Muff Cob	Kuril, Moskva, Kresta I and II, Poti, Grisha, Nanuchka, Ugra, Turya, Chilikin and Manych classes
57	70	Single (dual purpose)	85°	120	2·8	9,000	6,000	Hawk Screech	Skory (mod) and Sasha classes
45	85	Quadruple	90°	160	—	9,000	7,000	Hawk Screech	Kildin, Kotlin, Tallin
37	63	Twin	80°	130	—	4,000	3,000	Eye-shooting	Sverdlov, Chapaev, Skory (mod) and Riga classes
37	63	Single	80°	130	—	4,000	3,000	Eye-shooting	Skory (unmod), Kronstadt, T301 classes
30	65	Twin	85°	150	—	4,000	3,000	Drum Tilt or Muff Cob	Fast attack craft
30?	—	?	—	—	—	—	—	—	Note: A new form of point-defence system, possibly of a Gatling type. Kara and Kresta II classes
25	60	Twin	85°+	200	—	4,000	—	—	In enclosed or open mountings in smaller craft and gunboats
12·7	—	Twin	—	—	—	—	—	—	Close range weapons in smaller ships such as Kronstadt class

APPENDIX 3

SOVIET ANTI-SUBMARINE WEAPONS

Although Asroc entered USN service in 1960, Malafon was put to sea by France in 1962 and Ikara by Australia in 1966 the only long-range (10–12 miles) A/S weapon identified in the ships of the Soviet navy is the additional twin-arm launcher for a possible nuclear depth-bomb or torpedo in the "Moskva" class. In view of their interest in A/S warfare and the emphasis on this aspect in their ship-type names it seems strange that no further advance has apparently been made. In view, however, of the development of the USN's Mark 10 Mod 7 launcher which has a dual capability of firing Terrier or Asroc missiles and the later production of a similar launcher for the "Virginia" class cruisers firing Standard MR or Asroc missiles (both being stowed in the same magazine) it does seem possible that something like the same form of dual-purpose launcher may be amongst those fitted in certain Soviet ships. There is at present no evidence to support this suggestion but, were it true, it would significantly improve the A/S capability of the Soviet fleet which currently relies on the following rocket-firing weapons:

Number	No. of Tubes	Calibre	Range	Mounted in
MBU 1800	5	250-mm	1,800 m	Kronstadt and SO 1 classes
MBU 2500	12 or 16	300-mm	2,500 m	Cruisers, destroyers and frigates
MBU 4500	6	300-mm	2,500 m	Kara, Kresta I and II classes

Each projectile is reported as about 500 lb – this seems excessive.
Note: The Soviet Navy also carries both 21-inch and 16-inch torpedoes for A/S purposes, the former also having an anti-surface-ship capability.

APPENDIX 4

SOVIET NAVAL RADARS

Code Name	Freq. Band	Function	Ship Application
Ball End	E/F	Surface warning	Kola
Ball Gun	E/F	Surface warning	Kronstadt and older light forces
Big Net	C/D	Long-range air warning	Kresta I, Kashin (some), *Dzerzhinski*
Boat Sail	D or E	Surveillance	Whisky Canvas Bag
Cross Bird	G	Early warning	Obsolescent older destroyers
Dead Duck	G	IFF	General
Don-2	H/I	Navigation	–
Drum Tilt	H/I	Short-range armament Control	General with 30-mm guns
Egg Cup	E/F	Fire Control	–
Fan Song E	G	Control for SAN-2	*Dzerzhinski*
Flat Spin	D or E	Air surveillance	Some destroyers
Hair Net	E/F	Search & Surveillance	Kildins, Kotlins and frigates
Half Bow	I	Torpedo fire control	Older destroyers
Hawk Screech/ Owl Screech	G	Acquisition and fire control for main armament	Ships mounting 57–100-mm guns
Head Light	G/H/ I	Missile control	Most modern major surface ships
Head Net A	E/F	Air surveillance	Kynda, Kashin, Krupny and other destroyers
Head Net B	E/F	Air surveillance	Krupny (some)
Head Net C	E/F	Air surveillance and Height Finder	Kiev, Moskva, Kara, Kresta I and II and SAM-fitted destroyers
High Lune	E/F	Height finder	*Dzerzhinski* (with FanSong E)
High Pole	G	IFF	General
High Sieve	E/F	Surveillance	–
Horn Spoon	–	Navigation	General
Knife Rest	I	Air warning	Sverdlovs and Kildins
Long Bow	–	Torpedo fire control	Destroyers
Low Sieve	E/F	Surface search	–

Muff Cob	G/H/I	Fire control	Moskva, Kresta I and II, Ugra, Lama, Poti, T58, Polnocny, light forces
Neptune	H/I	Navigation	Light forces
Owl Screech (see *Hawk Screech*)			
Peel Group	H/I	SAN-1 fire control	Kresta I, Kashin, Kynda, SAM Kotlin, Kanin
Plinth Net	–	Surface search	Obsolete
Pop Group	H/I	Fire Control	Modern destroyers
Post Lamp	H/I	Fire Control	Older destroyers
Pot Drum	H/I	Surface search	Some light forces and Kronstadts
Pot Head	H/I	Surface search	Some light forces and Kronstadts
Round Top	–	Fire control system	Older destroyers
Scoop Pair	E	SSN-3 guidance	Kresta I and Kynda
Ship Globe	E	Missile Tracking	Instrumentation ships
Skin Head	H/I	Surface search	Some light forces and Krupny
Slim Net	E/F	Surface search	Some destroyers and frigates
Snoop Plate	H/I	Surveillance	Submarines
Snoop Slab	H/I	Surveillance	Submarines
Snoop Tray	H/I	Surveillance	Submarines
Square Head	G	IFF interrogator	Osa, Kotlin and Skory
Square Tie	H/I	Surface search	Osa
Strut Curve	E/F	Medium range search	Poti, Support ships
Sun Visor B	H/I	Fire control	–
Top Bow	H/I	Fire control	Some cruisers and destroyers
Top Sail	G	Air surveillance	Moskva, Kiev, Kara, Kresta II
Top Trough	E/F	Surface Search	Sverdlovs
Wasp Head	–	Fire control system	Older destroyers
Witch Five	G	IFF	Some cruisers and destroyers

APPENDIX 5

OCEAN SURVEILLANCE SATELLITES

Since December 1967 the Soviet Union has launched at least eleven satellites whose task appears to be ocean surveillance, a programme which is believed to be the largest such effort by any country. The exact form of these satellites has not been released although it is known that those launched during the last year have been larger than their predecessors. The sensors are presumably radar and photographic – with the advance in Soviet space technology real-time reporting would appear to be a probability. If a spacecraft can report the conditions on neighbouring planets it certainly seems likely that an up-to-the-minute picture can be received in Moscow from this pattern of eleven satellites. Stretching conjecture even further and again considering the reports transmitted by various spacecraft as well as Soviet interest in Elint (electronig intelligence) in their AGIs, it would also seem to be on the cards that some form of monitoring of both wireless and radar transmissions could be effected. Were this so, identification of the ships tracked by the satellites would be much facilitated. But both these possibilities are conjectual without any evidence to support them except for a study of modern Soviet capabilities.

Satellite number	Launch date
Cosmos 198	Dec. 27 1967
Cosmos 209	Mar. 22 1968
Cosmos 367	Oct. 3 1970
Cosmos 402	Apr. 1 1971
Cosmos 469	Dec. 25 1971
Cosmos 516	Aug. 21 1972
Cosmos 626	Dec. 27 1973
Cosmos 651	May 15 1974
Cosmos 654	May 17 1974
Cosmos 723	Apr. 2 1975
Cosmos 724	Apr. 7 1975
Cosmos 751	Jul. 23 1975
Cosmos 752	Jul. 24 1975
Cosmos 758	Sep. 5 1975

A study of these figures shows that, after a pattern became distinguishable, the average interval, except for the gap between Cosmos 516 and 626, has been about five to eight months until Cosmos 651. Two days later came 654 and after some eleven months Cosmos 723 was launched to be followed five days later by 724. It seems possible, therefore, that since May 1974 there may have been a dual capability available to Moscow, a possibility strengthened by the launching of Cosmos 751 and 752 in July 1975 at one day's interval.

FURTHER READING

Books

David Fairhall, *Russia Looks to the Sea*. A study of the expansion of
Soviet Maritime Power, London, 1971, 287 pp.

Michael McGwire (Ed.) *et al.*, *Soviet Naval Policy*. Objectives and
Constraints. Praeger Pub. (New York-London), 1975, 663 pp.

Donald W. Mitchell, *A History of Russian and Soviet Sea Power*,
London, 1974, 657 pp.
(Historical survey from the earliest days of Russian naval development
to the present).

Norman Polmar, *Soviet Naval Power*, London 1975, 126 pp.

Translations

S. G. Gorshkov (Admiral-of-the-Fleet of the Soviet Union): see Red
Star Rising at Sea. Navies in War and Peace.
(Ed. Col. Herbert Preston USMC), London 1975.
This is a translation of S. G. Gorshkov's series of articles "Voenno-
morskie floty v voinakh i mirnoe vremya", *Morskoi Sbornik* (1972–73).

Soviet publications

V. I. Achkasov and N. B. Pavlovich, *Sovetskoe voenno-morskoe
iskusstvo v Velikoi Otechestvennoi voine*, Moscow, Voenizdat, 1973,
404 pp.
(Compiled by two Soviet admirals, this study of Soviet naval operations
1941–45 is intended for senior officers and for use in military/naval
academies.

A. V. Basov (Chief Editor), *Boevoi put Sovetskogo Voenno-morskogo
Flota*, Moscow, Voenizdat, 1974 (3rd. Edn.), 592 pp.
(General history of the Soviet Navy).

S. Gorshkov (Admiral-of-the-Fleet of the Soviet Union),
"Nekotorye voprosy razvitiya voenno-morskogo iskusstva", *Morskoi Sbornik*, 1974, No. 12, pp. 24–32.
(Admiral Gorshkov on recent developments in naval tactics and organisation: an important article by the Soviet Navy's C-in-C).

Admiral V. M. Grishanov (Ed.), *Voina, Okean, Chelovek*, Moscow, Voenizdat, 1974, 232 pp.
(Admiral Grishanov is chief of the Political Administration/Soviet Navy: this handbook deals with political indoctrination and "psychological preparation" for Soviet naval personnel, including political work on long-distance cruises and in the Naval Air Force.

OKEAN, Moscow, Voenizdat, 1970, 208 pp.
(Description and photographs, Soviet naval manoeuvres "OKEAN", April–May 1970).

P. N. Ivanov, *Krylya nad morem*, Moscow, Voenizdat, 1973, 304 pp.
(General history of the Soviet Naval Air Force).

P. V. Kukushkin, *Batalon v morskom desante*, Moscow, Voenizdat, 1972, 176 pp.
(The battalion in an amphibious assault: for officers of the Ground Forces and for use in naval schools).

I. N. Potapov (Prof.), *Razvitie voenno-morskikh flotov v poslevoennyi period*, Moscow, Voenizdat, 1971, 292 pp.
(Post-war naval developments and building programmes in USA, Great Britain, W. Germany and Japan, analysed for Soviet naval officers).

S. N. Prasolov and M. B. Amitin, *Ustroistvo podvodnykh lodok*, Moscow, Voenizdat, 1973, 311 pp.
(A handbook on submarine design and construction for junior personnel and for use in naval schools).

V. D. Skugarev (Ed.), *Setevoe planirovanie na flote*, Moscow, Voenizdat, 1973, 248 pp.
(Handbook on network planning for naval purposes, including combat training, logistics, research: for naval officers, mercantile marine and fishing fleet officers, naval constructors corps).

V. D. Skugarev and K. O. Dubravin, *Nauka upravleniya i flot*, Moscow, Voenizdat, 1972, 216 pp.
(Textbook on control systems and "organisation and methods", OM, for naval officers).

A. O. Smukul and A. S. Fedurin, *Suda obespecheniya VMF*, Moscow, Voenizdat, 1969, 232 pp.
(An important textbook on supply and support ships, including afloat-support, for officers of the Soviet Navy and for the naval constructors corps).

A. O. Smukul and A. S. Fedurin, *Tyl voenno-morskikh sil*, Moscow, Voenizdat, 1973, 268 pp.
(Naval logistics, analysing the US Navy's experience and techniques for Soviet naval officers).

A. M. Vasilev *et al.*, *Morskie desantnye sily*, Moscow, Voenizdat, 1971, 288 pp.
(Outline of the development of amphibious forces for officers of the Soviet armed forces).

S. E. Zakharov, Admiral (Ed.), *Istoriya voenno-morskogo iskusstva*, Moscow, Voenizdat, 1969, 575 pp.
(Issued under the auspices of the Main Naval Staff as a standard text-book on naval strategy and tactics for naval schools).